PRAISE FOR SEEING ABILITY

I love how reading the book felt like I was sitting next to a supportive friend just talking about the ups and downs of parenting. I know it will be helpful to ALL parents—whether they have a kid with a disability or not. I am in the business of supporting parents, and this is going to be a great tool to help me do that.

—ALISON TYLER, HEAD OF SCHOOL, WALDEN SCHOOL

This book nails the most important thing to me as a doctor—the parent/provider partnership—with the parent as the team lead. Jim provides an excellent mix of practical advice and inspirational stories. I also agree with the advice to feel the emotions on this path. The book is a great resource for parents. It should be required reading for medical professionals.

—CHUCK DIETZEN, MD. AUTHOR, FOUNDER OF TIMMY GLOBAL HEALTH, FORMER CHIEF OF PEDIATRIC REHABILITATION MEDICINE AT RILEY HOSPITAL FOR CHILDREN AT IU HEALTH

I loved it! Even though the diagnoses differ, our journeys are similar and often intersect. Many of the quotes pulled from this book could have just as easily come from my own experiences. This book is so very needed and will be incredibly helpful to parents navigating a journey they did not plan for.

—SARAH RICHARDSON, EXECUTIVE DIRECTOR, SPINA BIFIDA ASSOCIATION OF KENTUCKY, MOTHER TO A DAUGHTER WITH SPINA BIFIDA

This book is a must-read for all parents on their life journey of raising a child with disabilities. I am a provider of services as well as a grandparent of two beautiful girls on the spectrum. This book will educate, inspire, and encourage our villages. We are not alone.

—SONIA JOHNSON, EXECUTIVE DIRECTOR, OPTIONS FOR INDIVIDUALS

Through sharing his own personal story of his daughter, Sophia, who was born prematurely with subsequent neurological issues, Jim provides new parents with all the right guideposts as they begin their journey of raising a child with significant challenges that threaten the child's future. Readable, comprehensive, relatable, and compassionate, this book is an essential reading for all parents of children with special needs. It was my good fortune as Sophia and Peter's pediatrician to share Jim's journey and see the evolution of his family, which became the basis for this book. Jim wisely and tenderly outlines the challenges and provides valuable advice and guidance to make the unmapped journey one of joy and discovery. I highly recommend this book and endorse his recommendations.

—RON LEHOCKY, MD, PEDIATRICIAN AND DISABILITY ADVOCATE

This book is a must-have for families of children with special needs, and maybe even more so for those who want to know what these families go through. Encouraging and informative. Nailed it!

—CAMERON HOWELL, PARENT TO MEDICALLY FRAGILE SON BROOKS, FINANCIAL SERVICES PROFESSIONAL

This book is real—real advice from real people who have found themselves dealing with unfamiliar and unexpected situations involving their greatest treasure: their child. While this book has an intended audience, the lessons taught are helpful in many different situations. When you find yourself in a place you didn't expect, ask questions, surround yourself with support of family, friends and professionals, stay as positive as you can, and don't forget what is truly important in life!

—JAMIE RAMSAY, PEDIATRIC PHYSICAL THERAPIST AT NORTON CHILDREN'S HOSPITAL AND KIDS CENTER FOR PEDIATRIC THERAPIES

When my son was diagnosed with sensory processing disorder, everything felt so overwhelming. I had to learn so much on my own; it would have been so helpful to have an encouraging book like this to aid us on our journey! As a community of parents come together to share their incredible stories, strength, hope, and faith for every child's future—no matter the challenges—are sure to be found among the pages.

—REBECCA DUVALL SCOTT, AUTHOR OF AWARD-WINNING, SPECIAL NEEDS SELF-HELP MEMOIR, *SENSATIONAL KIDS, SENSATIONAL FAMILIES: HOPE FOR SENSORY PROCESSING DIFFERENCES*

This book would be helpful to any parent or loved one, no matter where they are in their journey. It addresses the initial shock and emotional turmoil that come with a diagnosis or the realization of special needs, offering empathy and practical advice for navigating these feelings. For parents who are just starting to face these challenges, the shared experiences and reassurance that their emotions are valid can provide comfort and a sense of community. The book covers all stages, from the initial shock through every emotion you can think of, making it a valuable resource throughout the entire process. Whether a parent is at the beginning, middle, or further along in their journey, they can find relevant insights, support, and encouragement within its pages.

—CRIMSON CLAYCOMB, FOUNDER OF KENDYL & FRIENDS, A NONPROFIT FOCUSED ON INCLUSION FOR THOSE WITH DISABILITIES, MOTHER TO A CHILD WITH A DISABILITY

SEEING ABILITY

FINDING YOUR PATH IN PARENTING A CHILD
WITH SPECIAL NEEDS

JIM LITTLEFIELD-DALMARES

Seeing Ability: Finding Your Path in Parenting a Child with Special Needs

Copyright © 2024 by Jim Littlefield-Dalmares
Published by Possibility Publications (Kentucky)

All rights reserved. No portion of this book may be reproduced in any form or by electronic or mechanical means, including information storage and retrieval systems, without written permission of the author, except for the use of brief quotations in a book review.

Cover by Madelyn Copperwaite of MC Creative LLC
Editing by Jennifer Crosswhite of Tandem Services LLC
Layout by Stephanie Feger of emPower PR Group

First edition, September 2024
ISBN (Paperback): 979-8-9909640-0-6
Library of Congress Control Number: 2024914806
Created in the United States of America

Learn more about Jim Littlefield-Dalmares, his podcast, and the Seeing Ability Foundation, Inc. by visiting seeingability.com. Special discounts are available on quantity book purchases. Contact seeingability@gmail.com for information.

To every parent who joined a club they never expected.
To our Sophia, who taught us how to be parents.
To my rock and my forever sweetheart, LeAngela.
To my son Peter, who let us have a second try at parenting.
To my parents, who believed in me in everything I did, including my writing.
To the friends who encouraged me to write my first book.
To those in education, healthcare, and nonprofits who are champions of ability.
To those who travel the world each day with differing abilities.

CONTENTS

    Curveball   11
    A Book is Born   15

1. Acceptance   19
2. Navigating the World of Medicine   31
3. Put on Your Own Oxygen Mask   43
4. It Takes a Village   51
5. Dealing with Others   61
6. Family Impact   67
7. Setting the Bar   79
8. Advocating for Your Child's Education   91
9. The Road Less Traveled   101
10. Don't Stop Believin'   105

    Acknowledgments   111
    About the Author   113
    About the Seeing Ability Podcast   115
    About the Foundation   117
    Appendix 1   119
    Appendix 2   123

CURVEBALL

"I don't think we'll have to take the baby today."

The year was 2000, and we were expecting our first child. It was the one time I had not gone with my wife LeAnn to a prenatal appointment. I was on the planning team for an all-staff retreat at work that started the next day. Our final prep meeting was at the same time as the appointment. This was March, and the baby was not due until June, so missing one visit would surely be okay, right? Not exactly.

I GOT A CALL THAT I NEEDED TO DROP EVERYTHING.

My mind raced as I frantically drove to the hospital. Was the baby okay? What about LeAnn? I had no idea what to expect, but I knew something was wrong, and it was serious. The next few days were overwhelming. I never did make it to that retreat!

"I don't think we'll have to take the baby today." Those were the words the doctor said to my wife, LeAnn, and I not long after I arrived. While the doctor may have uttered other words, I can promise you I did not hear any of them.

Twenty-five weeks pregnant, LeAnn had noticed severe swelling in her legs, which was attributed to the flight back from overseas a few days before. What we didn't know was the swelling was merely a symptom of a larger issue, and she had trouble brewing inside her body. When the nurses conducted their routine prenatal checks—documenting her weight and blood pressure—they saw what the naked eye couldn't and knew quickly she needed immediate care. LeAnn had preeclampsia, a condition that threatens mother and baby and is cured by immediate delivery. Our journey to parenthood quickly shifted from Hallmark movie expectations.

One thing can happen in your life, and suddenly nothing else matters. You start your day thinking of what is going on at work or what you have coming up for the weekend. You might have trouble sleeping because of a deadline or not be able to take your mind off a conflict you had with a friend or family member. As an adult, you quickly realize life is not about trying to find a moment of calm seas with the absence of stress. Instead, adulthood is about learning how to ride the waves of work and family life.

Then there are those seminal moments—the ones you cannot just remember but can feel twenty years later, where everything can change.

Hours before this news I was a thirty-two-year-old, happily married man, passionate about my work, fresh off a European vacation. We were enjoying the "home stretch" of the journey you go on when you are expecting your first child. Sophia would also be the first grandchild on both sides of our family. To say we were giddy with anticipation and joy would be the understatement of the year. We had read *What to Expect When You're Expecting* and were making all the plans.

SOPHIA'S BIRTH WAS NOT A TYPICAL CELEBRATION.

It felt more like a car crash. Imagine driving down a road, top down on a sunny day, favorite music playing, smiling, singing along, en route to a fun party. Then out of nowhere, your car is hit. Everything seems to move in slow-motion. You are thrown through the air, and all you can hear is a loud buzzing that drowns out the world. Everything around you is a blur.

That is what it felt like that day I rushed to meet my wife and unborn baby at the hospital.

Over the next few days, we tried to delay Sophia's birth, buying as much time as possible. Every day in utero means more steps of development for the baby. After two days, it was time for a C-section. I navigated a weird mix of emotions. On one hand, my wife was terribly sick, and the only cure for her was to deliver the baby. On the other hand, delivering a baby so early meant great risks. I remember getting into scrubs, and even though I was terrified, I also felt that proud new dad energy. After all, this was the birth of my baby girl.

> And then for an instant in the delivery room, all that stress melted away as I saw the doctor lift Sophia out of her mother and into this world. Delivery also meant that LeAnn would be just fine.

That relief quickly turned to worry as I went alone to meet our baby. LeAnn could not even see her, because she was still in bed recovering from her condition and the emergency C-section. Sophia came into the world on March 4, 2000, at twenty-six weeks. She weighed just one pound, eight ounces and was clinging to life.

I can easily recall the first time I saw Sophia in the Neonatal Intensive Care Unit (NICU). If you've never been around the earliest of preemies, it's hard to get a sense of just how incredibly small they are. I could cup her entire head in the palm of my hand. Her legs were the width of my index finger; her hands and fingers smaller than the tiniest doll you could imagine. My precious little girl was so, so fragile and delicate. She was under a heat lamp, her eyes covered by what looked like a miniature sleep mask and her body clothed in a covering that reminded me of Saran Wrap you'd use to cover leftovers when reheating in the microwave. Her skin was pasty, and the visible hair she had up and down her arms and legs reminded me of feathers on a baby bird. She looked like a porcelain doll, beautiful to the eye but breakable upon touch. A maze of wires came out of her body, and the constant ringing of monitors created her own, and likely unwelcomed, white noise. Sophia had a tube down her throat so a ventilator could pump air in and out of her tiny lungs since she was unable to breathe on her own.

It was a lot for anyone to take in, especially a first-time parent. Everything I hoped and dreamed for my little girl lay in limbo, her life included. Our journey to parenthood didn't come with tears of joy; it was filled with tears of the unknown. We were on a parenting path we never expected.

We had been inducted into a group of parents who are raising kids with disabilities. It's not a club most seek to join. However, I have come to learn from years of being a member that it's a village of passionate people who are willing to pay it forward so other parents can learn from the knowledge they have gained in the trenches.

A BOOK IS BORN

When most people are expecting their first child, they go through many stages to get ready. This might include a lot of reading, preparing the house, taking classes, and much more. But I have yet to meet a parent whose gift registry included a walker, wheelchair, or communication device. There is literally no manual on how to travel this path. Despite the best prenatal preparations, you are jolted into an entirely new challenge, like being tossed into the ocean without a life vest. Nobody is prepared for it.

In those early days when Sophia was clinging to life, unable to breathe on her own, I turned to writing to find some solace. I posted a piece online titled "A Breath for Sophia." It was a sort of prayer to the world to help my tiny daughter get through this crucial period in her life. The response was overwhelming, with so many parents relating to the struggle. We got email messages from other countries and met many parents who had also been thrust into this world. This experience showed me the power of the written word and its ability to connect a community of people traveling this path in silence and often in isolation.

Not long after Sophia was born, I started working at the Kids Center for Pediatric Therapies, the place where she went for physical therapy to help with her mobility and occupational therapy to help with her fine motor skills. The Center became a home away from home for us. My job was in marketing and fundraising, which gave me a unique opportunity to connect with fellow parents and learn their stories. I produced a quarterly newsletter, and the cover story for each issue was about one of the kids we served and their families.

Over the next ten years, about forty families got to know me, let me in, and gave me a window into their world.

The range of issues they faced in terms of diagnosis was vast. But what I found were amazing similarities in the challenges they faced and the strength and resilience they showed as parents. I realized the collective experience of this group could help others. There was gold in their strategies, mindsets, resilience, and lessons learned the hard way.

I GOT THE IDEA TO WRITE A BOOK THAT WOULD NOT ONLY SHARE MY STORY, BUT WOULD ALSO INCORPORATE THE LEARNINGS OF OTHERS.

Together, we could produce something that would bring comfort and value to the next parent whose journey turned from Hollywood to a different type of story.

I set out to interview a variety of people in this community. I've talked with over a hundred people to find out what they felt, what they learned, and what they wish someone had told them early in their journey. I've spoken with parents of children with disabilities and adults who grew up navigating that journey themselves. I've chatted with founders of nonprofits, medical doctors supporting various disabilities, special-education teachers, and a variety of types of therapists all who use their God-given talents to help families like mine navigate the unknown. Throughout my own quest to uncover what I wish I had known when receiving the hard news as a first-time parent, consistent themes began surfacing, which inspired me to dig deeper.

My goals for this book include:

- **Education**: In each chapter, expect to gather ideas, tips, and strategies that could help you support your child.
- **Motivation**: When I hear stories of others who overcome adversity, it always gives me a burst of emotion, a bit of inspiration, and a lot of motivation to stay the course. My hope is that these stories do the same for you.
- **Community**: Nobody gets it quite like another parent traveling the same path.

When you read this book, I want it to feel like home. You are a part of a new community you never knew existed, and you are not alone.

1 ACCEPTANCE

Every path for a parent raising a child with some type of challenge is different. But many start with a bit of pure shock. Think of a typical newborn gift registry. You are going to see a stroller, car seat, and baby monitor on most lists. What you won't see is a feeding tube, a wheelchair, braces, or a communication device. Everything you thought you knew does not matter. You suddenly realize that your beautiful child is going to face so many hardships. It hits you like a ton of bricks. And there is no way around the pain and range of emotions you feel as a parent. The first step for most special needs parents is to find a way through the shock so you can move forward as a family.

RECOGNIZE THE EMOTION AND BE OKAY FEELING IT

We all have the image of what LeAnn and I used to call the "Hollywood delivery." You know, the one where the adoring family sits in the waiting room awaiting the birth of the newest family member. Dad comes out, dressed in scrubs, taking off his mask to reveal an ear-to-ear grin as he announces the birth of their child to the family, filling the room with tears of joy, hugs, and celebration among generations.

Ours was definitely *not* the Hollywood experience.

In the days leading up to Sophia's birth, I thought I could lose them both. That feeling shook me to the core. Then, when she was born, I was flooded with two competing emotions. First, I was elated with the fact that she and my wife survived. At the same time, I felt tremendous worry and uncertainty about her future. I will never forget our "celebration meal" in the hospital. What should have been pure joy for us was a time to hold each other, cry, and lean on each other to find the strength to face the days ahead. We had no idea what was ahead. We were not even sure we had the strength to face it.

Not everyone's birth journey begins in the NICU. Some have a more "typical" delivery experience but later notice issues their child faces as they grow, possibly missing developmental milestones. For them, the car crash comes at the time of a diagnosis. Regardless of when it hits, it can feel like you're met with a tsunami of emotions.

> Like an episode of *The Twilight Zone*, everything you thought you knew gets turned on its head, the world seems to spin fast, and it's easy to get a little dizzy.

The fight or flight reflexes kick in, and we become so focused on taking care of our child we never stop to take stock of the emotions we are experiencing. Without exception, the number one piece of advice I got from all parents was that it's important to stop, to *feel* those emotions, and to know it's okay to feel them. Let me repeat myself here—it is *okay* to have these emotions, and it is *okay* to feel them.

The emotions, worry, and fear come in all forms. See if you can relate to this list of feelings and thoughts when you found yourself at this place.

- You are mad at the world and at God, and you are confused as to why this is even happening.

- You've asked yourself, "Why did this happen to me and to my child?"
- You're angry you took all the precautions and tried to do everything right during your pregnancy, yet still ended up with issues.
- You are starting to imagine your child will never play sports, you will never watch them from the stands, or be their Little League coach.
- You feel like you are to blame for your child's disability.
- You feel depressed and overwhelmed. You are not sure you are up to the job and wonder if you can do it.

You are not alone. Every parent on this path has felt the same way. It is natural. It's okay to have *all* these feelings. But on top of this heavy list of feelings, most of us add guilt. We don't just feel bad, we also feel *bad* or *guilty* we are even feeling this way.

It's important not to feel bad or guilty. So many parents feel sad because of the loss of the child they thought they would have. Then on top of that they also feel incredible guilt, like they are a bad person for even feeling this way. Honor what you are feeling without judgment.

Find a way to process these emotions. Many parents found solace in journaling and putting their feelings on paper. In fact, in doing research for this book, I met several parents who are authors and dozens more who say they have a book in them. Put it down in writing. This helps you get in touch with how you feel.

It also may be important to consider some type of therapy or mental health services. In most states, there is an early intervention program that brings therapists to the home to work with the child. But many I spoke with suggested it would be great if there were services focused on the emotional state of the parents and their ability to adjust to what it means to be a parent in this world. Whether it's talking to a qualified mental health professional, talking to your spouse or significant other, talking to a friend, leaning on your faith, or journaling—get in touch with your emotions and the feelings washing over you.

It's critical for all partners to identify the root of what they are feeling. Create a safe space for everyone to acknowledge their emotions. "It was hard for me to get in touch with my real feelings, because as the man of the house, I am always supposed to be in control," added Brad Meshell. "I was lucky that my wife gave me the space and support to be vulnerable and admit that I was hurting." Being there for each other at the beginning and giving a lot of grace cannot be emphasized enough.

RISE ABOVE WORRY. TAKE THINGS ONE DAY AT A TIME.

When Sophie was in the hospital, our main concern was the here and now. But it was also hard not to worry about her future. I would find myself going down a rabbit hole of the worst-case scenarios for her future. For most parents who find their child has a disability, often even before a formal diagnosis, you run the risk of racing ahead to worry about their future. Will they ever have a job? Will they find friends? Will they be picked on or bullied at school? Will they get married? I was right there, asking all those questions in my mind. If you find yourself asking these questions, then good news: You're like many parents in this situation. It's normal to hold your infant in your arms and suddenly fast-forward to imagine all the hardships they will face that you wish you could somehow help them avoid.

> Connecting to the larger community of people who have faced similar challenges can bring context, peace, and hope.

You will find you worry less when you connect with another parent whose child had faced a similar road and had made it through. One parent I spoke with said they were stuck on all the things their child would not do. But when they had the chance to talk to other parents who had adult children with the same condition, it gave them hope their child could get through anything.

Parenting does not come with guarantees. While some kids may seem to have a clear and easy path, any parent will tell you that is far from the truth. Ask the parent whose teen became addicted to drugs or who buried their teenager after suicide, and you realize an easy path for any child is just an illusion.

One way to worry less about the future is to learn to be present and appreciate today. Don't become so focused on the diagnosis and what's "wrong" with your child that you forget to enjoy having a child and let them be a kid. While it sounds cliché to say stop and smell the roses, that is what many parents wished they'd done more of. "Instead of worrying about whether they'd go to college, I wish we had just played in the rain more," added one mother. By resisting the temptation to spiral into negative thinking about what-ifs for their future life, start each day by planning to make that day as good as possible.

DON'T DENY GRIEF. EXPERIENCE IT AND MOVE ON.

It's important to realize and be okay with the fact that you are grieving the life you thought your child would have. You might be the dad who saw yourself playing catch with your son in the backyard and sitting in the stands at their first Little League game. Maybe you are the mom who loves to sing and imagines your daughter discovering her love of the stage at an early age.

Perhaps you are the academic who imagines yourself in the audience as your child takes the stage wearing a cap and gown to give their speech as valedictorian.

Whatever your vision was, there is a feeling of grief as you sit with what the future may hold. It's important to recognize it, feel it, and honor how real it is. It's also important to realize you are not just grieving the life you thought your child would have, but the life you saw *yourself* having too. This is normal. Uncomfortable? Sure. Healthy? Yes.

Not processing grief can have lasting impacts. One nonprofit founder shared the story of an adult child with spina bifida whose mother still cried every time she heard someone say spina bifida. Imagine how painful it was for that mother to feel such sadness that every time she even heard the name of her child's diagnosis it immediately made her cry. Then stop to imagine how damaging it was for her daughter to know that some part of her identity brought her mother to tears. It was as if just who she was became a source of pain for that mother. This story shows how damaging it can be to not address and work through the grief of this journey.

Grief is not a one-time event.

Raising a child has stages and seasons—birth to school age, lower school, adolescence, and so on. Each stage comes with new opportunities and challenges, and you should not be surprised if a wave of grief and emotions floods you at multiple stages. This might be the time you realize that nobody calls your child to play on the weekends. It might be the loss of some friends who can't relate to your daily experience. It might be the realization that your nest may never be empty. There will be emotions and grief at many stages beyond just birth or initial diagnosis. But there is good news. When you have learned to get through the first wave of grief, it will make recovery from future waves shorter and a lot less painful.

LET GO OF GUILT

Even though medically it's very rare that anything could have been prevented, parents still often feel as if their child's disability is their fault. One mother blamed herself for her daughter's disability until she was five years old and doctors finally convinced her otherwise.

This hit hard for my wife LeAngela. As a first-time parent, she tried to do things by the book. When our happy pregnancy turned into a medical emergency, LeAnn found herself wondering what she could have done differently to carry Sophia to term. It was almost as if she felt she had failed the assignment to take care of Sophia until she was ready to be born.

To move forward, we have to find a way to acknowledge and feel both grief and guilt. Then we must find the courage to let them go. There is no easy way to do this. Parents I spoke with recommended journaling and support groups. Others relied on a faith community. Nearly everyone found solace by talking to other parents who had been in their shoes. Many found peace by seeking the help of a qualified mental health professional.

LOVE YOUR CHILD AS THEY ARE AND STOP TRYING TO FIX THINGS

When your child has a disability or delay, it's very easy to focus on what is wrong, the deficits, the milestones they are not hitting.

When I asked a mother of a twenty-nine-year-old with Down syndrome about the one thing she wished someone had told her early on, she replied, "To forget her diagnoses and to just love my child as if they were my perfect child."

Wanting your child to have the best life possible and grow into a productive and happy adult is understandable. It's what we all want for our children.

> But what if instead of approaching each day as a battle to tackle what is wrong, you set a goal to make each day a great day and to help your child take a step toward the goal of adult independence?

"I caught myself asking God to make Nate normal," explained Colleen Payne, whose son has spina bifida. "Then I stopped and asked myself what kind of goal is that anyway? My life totally changed the day I decided to stop trying to fix my child and realized he was perfect just as he was. My goal became to help Nate become the best version of himself today—and that made all the difference moving forward."

EMBRACE THE NEW PATH AHEAD

To give you a real sense of perspective, I strongly recommend you read "Welcome to Holland," an essay written in 1987 by American author and social activist Emily Pearl Kingsley. It's a profound, relatable essay with a message that says even though this is not *at all* what you prepared for or expected, it can still turn out to be beautiful and pretty amazing. If you have not read it, stop right now and find it before you come back to this page. Save it. You might need to refer to it more than once.

The road of raising a child with unique abilities will bring you gifts you did not expect. It will allow you to see the world through a different lens. It will bring you a path filled with triumph, joy, heartache, and laughter. You will discover strengths you didn't know you possessed and encounter deep love and support. You will meet people who will extend your community and give you strength. While I don't normally advise reading ahead, if you'd like a little burst of inspiration, feel free to flip to chapter ten, where I share story after story of children who have beat the odds and experienced the joys this path has brought to their families.

There is no denying the challenges ahead. Those are real, but with the right tools and mindset, you can take on each challenge better prepared. When you can recognize your emotions, stop worrying, experience grief, let go of guilt, and accept your child as they are, you are now ready to accept and even welcome the road ahead.

A PROBLEM YOU CAN'T JUST FIX

When Brad Meshell was in his late thirties, he was resigned to the idea that he might stay "single Brad" and never get married. He definitely did not see himself becoming a father. But when he met Jamie, he soon found himself married at age forty and expecting a baby within a few months. He was so elated at the idea of becoming a father that he rushed home and painted what looked more like a small man cave than a typical nursery. Soon they welcomed a bouncing baby boy named Jacob, and Brad was over the moon with joy.

He marveled at this new chapter in his life. "How can they let you take something that tiny home with you," he thought. As a first-time dad, he had plenty of anxiety, even going in at night to watch Jacob sleep for the first several weeks.

Over the next year to year and a half, there were signs small and large that Jacob was not progressing. Jamie noticed he didn't look at them when they changed his diaper. He was on the clumsy side and walked on his toes. He wasn't talking very much and had way fewer words in his vocabulary than milestones called for. He also would not engage in contact or interaction unless someone else initiated it.

Brad would write these off as "just Jacob" for most of that period. When his mother-in-law suggested the possibility of autism, he got angry. Finally, Jamie convinced Brad that Jacob needed to get into some therapies. Brad agreed, but he was reluctant to pursue a diagnosis.

"I was okay with therapy, because that would not hurt him," he explained. "But I did not want him to have something really wrong with him."

When they finally agreed to get Jacob formally evaluated for autism, they were on a six-month waitlist, which created more fear and anxiety. Luckily, they were fast-tracked with an offer from Vanderbilt University to do some filming of their case. It didn't last long. They saw what they needed to see after just ten minutes of playing with Jacob. They were told it would be several weeks before the write-up.

Brad stopped the doctor. "I know you need to do your write-up and can't give us a formal answer on the spot. I get that. But I just need to know." The doctor simply nodded his head in the affirmative. Jacob was on the spectrum.

As they left with Jacob and put him into their van, Brad remembered his reaction to this news. "I could not breathe. I could not see. We cried. What did it mean for my son to have autism? And immediately I started to play out his life and think of all the things he would never be able to do. It was as if my life, and even Jacob's life, was over—or at least the life that I was expecting for both of us." The timing of this diagnosis was unusual because just as they were learning what was going on with Jacob, Jamie was expecting their second son, Jackson.

The evaluation happened in June, and baby Jackson was due in August. Brad found himself awash with emotions and going to a dark place of worry and isolation. "I didn't know how to handle it, to be honest. As a father and a man, you are supposed to provide for your family and protect them. As guys, we fix stuff. But I had no idea how to fix this, because it wasn't something Jacob would grow out of." He started to pull away and become less involved with both of his boys.

> For Brad, the path out of the grief and pain of Jacob's diagnosis was through action.

"I had always been active in sports and leadership. And somehow, I knew that I just needed to do something. So much of my life seemed out of control that I needed to do something that would help me take control over what was next," explained Brad. That action was a walk—a 444-mile walk, to be exact. In the winter of 2022, Brad decided he would walk the entire length of the Natchez Trace, which runs from Mississippi to Nashville and spans 444 miles. And he would do that walk in thirty days during the month of April to coincide with autism awareness month.

The walk spawned a charity named Jacob's Audible, after his son, which Brad runs today. Their mission is to raise awareness, provide education, and focus on parent support. "I knew I had to decide to step up and join Jacob and my family on a path that we never intended to take. I had to become part of a club I never intended to join. That is why our main focus is parent support. I know what it is like to feel like your world is over. I know what it is like to feel like nobody else understands. I know what it is like to feel lost. Luckily, I was able to come out of a very dark place. And I want to make sure other parents have that support when they need it along the journey." To learn more about Jacob's Audible, go to www.jacobsaudible.org.

2 NAVIGATING THE WORLD OF MEDICINE

When you have a child with special needs, you are going to see a *lot* of doctors. It's a part of every special needs parent's journey to figure out how to find your voice so you can navigate the world of medicine.

Sophia spent the first ten weeks of her life in the hospital. The Neonatal Intensive Care Unit, or NICU, is a wonderful yet terrifying place. Imagine a sci-fi movie with an infectious disease lab. Each day we would put on a gown and gloves to enter the ward. Sophia lay in a tiny box called an isolette. Multiple wires came out of her, and a constant hum of monitors filled the air. The consistent pulse of the monitors was somewhat calming—until an alarm went off, triggering a rush of nurses to the bedside and a burst of adrenaline rushing through us.

At one and a half pounds, Sophia was considered a micro-preemie. In neonatal medicine, there is a fine balance doctors face where every medical intervention they perform to fix one issue runs the risk of a consequence that could trigger a new problem. In her ten weeks, Sophia faced several forks in the road where we had to decide on treatment. For example, she was born with an eye condition called R.O.P., or retinopathy of prematurity. It's the same condition that led Stevie Wonder to become blind. Had Sophia been born a year earlier, she'd likely be blind today. Luckily, she was able to take advantage of a new laser surgery that gave her the gift of sight. Although she is not blind, she wears very thick lenses.

The NICU was a period of challenges but also of small victories.

It was hard for Sophia to breastfeed, so that meant constant pumping and freezing of breastmilk for LeAnn. Because Sophia initially did not breathe on her own, we constantly watched her oxygen saturation, often referred to as her "sats." Unlike most babies, we did not get to hold Sophia very often. Each time we pulled her out of her incubator to be held or to feed her, we'd run the risk of her sats dropping and alarms going off.

One of our favorite experiences in the NICU came with something called Kangaroo Care. Researchers had found a positive impact on preemies in the NICU when they would be held with skin-to-skin contact. This meant we got to take Sophia out on her isolette, wires and all, and hold her on our chest with skin-to-skin contact. At a time when so much was scary and stressful, I will never forget the peace, the calm, and the hope this time together brought to both of us. And while tiny infants at that age do not really smile, I swear we have a video of Sophia on my chest where I pretend to snore, and as I slowly release the sound in an exaggerated way, I swear that little girl smiled every time.

The NICU was indeed a scary place, but it was also filled with great love. One time we even "caught" our favorite nurse rocking Sophia. How comforting it felt that the staff there gave her such love.

Parents are confronted with complex issues, medical jargon, and forks in the road where decisions must be made. It's a quick master class course in the diagnosis of your child and how to communicate with your medical team. With some heightened awareness, organization, and perspective, I feel you can have a less stressful journey that will be better for you, your child, and their future.

BECOME THE EXPERT IN YOUR CHILD'S DIAGNOSIS

We are blessed with amazing doctors and other medical staff who dedicate their lives to helping others. But they are not all specialists in your child's diagnosis. To advocate for your child, you need a crash course in what you are facing. Read as much as you can to learn about your child's issues.

But beware—there is such a thing as reading too much and sending yourself into a spiral of worry and confusion. Think of times that you or someone you know has gone to "Dr. Google," and a rash on their body suddenly had them convinced they had every type of cancer known to humans. This can be very unproductive. Be careful not to go so deep into the diagnosis that all you can see are the obstacles and the worst-case scenarios.

One mother shared the best thing she did for herself upon receiving a diagnosis was to take a brief leave from work. This allowed her to dedicate the time to research and sent a clear message to her friends and coworkers that she was dealing with something very serious. It also gave her time to process her emotions and feelings on that acceptance journey. While this may not be financially feasible for everyone, the idea of taking some type of intentional pause at the onset of the journey is a great one.

Get a general understanding of what your child is facing so you can be more at peace with the road ahead. The last thing you want is for your research to have the opposite effect. Here are some tips.

- *Start with organizations that support your diagnosis.* Whether you're exploring Down syndrome, autism, spina bifida, or cerebral palsy, many organizations will be able to provide you with a general overview of the challenges posed by your diagnosis. These organizations can point you in the direction of

resources, articles, and information. They also can often point you to others who have been in your shoes.
- *Get a translator.* The entire outlook of the medical part of the journey changed dramatically if the person I was talking to was a nurse, a therapist, a doctor, or had one of these professionals in the family. Reach out to someone in your family or your friend network who is in medicine so they can help you understand terminology and even help you know what type of questions to ask. Think of being faced with a complicated legal matter and asking an uncle who was an attorney for some context.
- *Ask others.* There have always been communities of people who are in the same or similar boat as you, but in the past, it was harder to connect to them than it is now. For all the downsides of the internet and social media, knowledge sharing is one of the blessings of the digital age. Whether it's a Facebook group or a TikTok video, there are great resources out there to arm yourself with knowledge. "It is amazing how you can feel close to people you have never met who share a very narrow niche in this world. It's not uncommon for a mom whose child uses a feeding tube to get an answer from another feeding-tube mom from a group at two a.m. This helped me so much to have others who have been there," added Denise Sims, whose daughter is medically complex and uses a feeding tube.

BE PREPARED FOR WHAT YOU MIGHT HEAR FROM DOCTORS

If you talk to many people on this path, you are surely going to hear stories of things a parent was told their child would never do. I once was told a story about a mother who years later saw a doctor at a restaurant and proudly marched over to share how wrong they were and throw their child's accomplishments in their face.

These emotions are very real. I get it. When Sophie was in the NICU, we had two great neonatologists that we affectionately referred to as "good cop" and "bad cop." The good cop was the one who would put their arm around you and comfort you. The bad cop was the one who told you the risks of every intervention and how we should temper expectations of what might be possible.

I believe it's important to start with a partnership mindset with your providers. This is not an adversarial relationship. In fact, if it feels that way, you should factor that into your choice of provider.

Try not to shoot the messenger, and have context for how medical people present things for your child. They all mean well, wanting to set realistic expectations, and they tend to fear presenting too rosy a picture and creating false hope. Do not put them on such a pedestal that you cannot question their advice. Most importantly, if they tell you about limits or challenges, accept them as input but not as a destined reality for your child. It's important to not set limits on what is possible for your child.

ASK QUESTIONS UNTIL YOU UNDERSTAND

It takes most parents a while to figure out how to have a healthy partnership with their medical team. In the beginning, you often do not fully understand but do not want to feel stupid by constantly asking questions. The exception to this, again, occurs among those with a medical background or who had a close friend or family member with a medical background present as their advocate every step of the way. Assuming you don't have that medical translator and warrior by your side, the single biggest challenge is that you do not fully understand what the medical team is saying, but you are afraid to ask questions.

It's okay and good to ask questions, but sometimes you don't really know what to ask. Find someone who has been in your shoes or works with this population and ask them what you should be asking. For example, often the care of your child comes to a fork in the road and a decision. This might be to have a surgery or procedure to address a problem. It can appear that the two choices are to do the surgery or not. But what most people don't know to ask is whether there is a third option to do something else. Doctors do not typically provide you with two or three choices. They present the treatment that they feel is best.

This makes sense because they likely don't want to confuse you with other things you "could do" if they truly feel, in this example, that surgery is best.

> Knowing that in an A or B choice, you can ask if there is an option C is a good example of how sometimes we don't know what we do not know.

Even if you ask questions, some medical people are not good at explaining things in lay terms. Keep asking until you fully understand. Try laying the groundwork that you are going to keep asking questions until you can repeat what is going on back to your provider in a way that makes sure you both are confident that you understand what is going on.

YOU ARE THE COORDINATOR OF YOUR CHILD'S CARE

Along this journey, you will encounter many very smart and caring medical professionals who will be invaluable to you and your family. They have studied these conditions, and they go by what they have learned, what they have seen, and how the diagnosis tends to present itself most of the time. In our society, it's very common to defer to medical experts. But the one person who knows your child best is *you*. The medical experts are not with them every day. You know them best. You need to own that and trust that.

The lead role is *not* the doctor or therapist. The lead coordinator in your child's medical care needs to be *you*. And in that statement, I am implying *both of you* if you are a couple. We are trained to defer to our medical providers.

That said, never forget that *you* are not the patient. When you see your small child hooked up to machines, undergoing painful procedures, and so on, your emotions can be so strong it can feel like you are the one on the table. It's key to separate yourself so you can be the "Coordinator of Care" and not the patient.

MEDICINE IS A CONSUMER RELATIONSHIP. YOU HIRE AND FIRE PROVIDERS.

Doctors and other medical professionals play such a critical role in this journey. I am friends with many doctors and have great respect for the time and dedication they put into their work. So many are in medicine as true healers and approach their work with passion and humility. The time and effort doctors put into their professional journey is truly impressive.

But we don't want to be so admiring of them that we have to blindly follow anything they say to the point it is almost sacrosanct to question them.

> It is one hundred percent okay to ask to get a second opinion when facing big choices.

A lot of people worry that will offend their provider. It won't. Or at least it shouldn't, and if it does, that might be a reason for pause. Any parent I spoke with who had regrets concerning medicine was typically that they had gone ahead with a medical path in spite of a gut feeling and wished they had gotten a second opinion.

Do not forget to consider looking outside your area. This is especially true if you live in a smaller or more rural area that might not experience your particular issue or have experts who specialize in the care. But even in larger cities, you still might pursue answers elsewhere.

It's critical for you to mesh well with your team. Caring for your child should be a team approach, and you should be recognized as the leader where your voice is heard and made to feel important. If you do not feel like your voice counts, you should probably consider getting a different provider.

LEARN TO GET THE MOST OUT OF MEDICAL APPOINTMENTS

In addition to having the right mindset when it comes to working with the medical community, there are also some very practical skills you can learn that will help you get more out of every single doctor's appointment. Here are some tips offered by those I spoke with:

Make it personal.

- Make sure they know you, your child, and your family.
- Get to know them and ask about their family.
- Modern medicine can be a bit like an assembly line. There are time and financial pressures to move through each appointment. You can be less of a "number" if you develop a personal connection to your providers.

You can't be too organized.

- You will want to keep detailed records of all appointments, diagnoses, providers, tests, insurance records, and so on.
- Even though we live in a digital age, most parents recommended a binder with sections for providers, visits, tests, diagnoses, and so on.
- Many parents pull key information from their medical binder and create one for caregivers.

Dress the part.

- Many reported that their questions and concerns were taken more seriously if they and their kids were well dressed, clean, hair done, and so on.

Consider taking a second person.

- Each appointment runs the risk of bad news. Whether you tend to be super emotional or not, hearing bad news can make it hard to process other information in a meeting. An objective party who is less impacted by the situation can take notes and possibly even prompt questions.

Prep before you go.

- Come in with a set of questions.
- Ask others if you do not know what to ask.

IF IT DOES NOT FEEL RIGHT, IT PROBABLY IS NOT RIGHT.

Without a doubt, the single biggest piece of advice when I asked people about their medical journey was to "trust your gut." LeAnn and I know all too well about this dynamic. When we returned from a trip to Italy, LeAnn was incredibly swollen. Even though we attributed some of this to an overseas flight, she was having extreme headaches and nausea. She was scheduled for her next prenatal visit on Wednesday, but we called the doctor's office on Monday worried that something was very wrong. They told her to not worry, that the swelling was likely from the flight and that everything would be fine.

Two days later, she went for that prenatal visit and within minutes was rushed to the hospital because her condition was so severe. Had we gone two days earlier, I'm not sure if it would have changed anything about Sophie's premature birth. But I do know we should have insisted that she be seen when our gut said she was very, very sick.

> We know firsthand what it's like to ignore those instincts. Do not ignore them.

Trust what your intuition is telling you and act accordingly. I do not think a single one of my one hundred interviews neglected to give this advice.

TRUSTING YOUR GUT

Sarah Richardson's daughter, Avery, was diagnosed with spina bifida upon birth and underwent several surgeries in her first days of life. When she came home, even though her hair was growing back from the place where her head had been shaved to insert a shunt, her mother had concerns about the veins on her forehead. She would gently run her fingers across her head and wonder if the veins were more prominent than the day before. She took pictures and sent them to other parents. "Does this look normal to you?" she asked.

Next, she noticed a burst blood vessel in Avery's eye. She talked herself out of going right to the neurologist and instead left a message for the nurse on their help line. When they got back to her, they asked a series of questions. They asked if Avery was sleeping well, was more irritable, or was having trouble keeping food down. Satisfied with those answers, they said not to worry, that nothing was wrong.

But in her gut, Sarah felt there could be an issue with Avery's shunt, and she called the neurology office three more times. They told her that blond babies often had visible veins and that burst blood vessels in the eye were common and not related to a shunt malfunction. Even though her doctor was out of town, the office finally set up an MRI to see what was going on, even though it would likely be a few weeks before they would be scheduled to see the doctor to follow up on the results.

At the test, the techs played with Avery, who appeared on the outside as a healthy baby. On the drive home, Sarah called to find out the results of the test. They were only two streets away from their house and were asked to immediately turn around, head back to the hospital, and to be sure to enter through the emergency room. When another doctor reviewed the test, they quickly realized that Avery's shunt had malfunctioned, and the ventricles in her brain were swelling with excess fluid.

Had Sarah not trusted her gut and insisted on a test, irreparable damage would have been done. "I felt a great sense of vindication for my concerns but also angry that I had to advocate so hard for them to be heard."

In countless interviews, I heard stories where concerned parents had their fears downplayed by doctors. To be fair, doctors likely do get a lot of calls from nervous parents who can make a mountain out of nothing. However, false alarms and overblown concerns should not cloud being able to see real problems. Many times, these concerns are real and are very well founded.

You need to take ownership of the idea that, while medical people study conditions and have experience, nobody knows your child quite as well as you. This gut feeling dilemma not only goes for initial concerns, but for decisions you will need to make when you come to a fork in the road and must choose a course of treatment. If you feel something is wrong, there is not a person on the planet better qualified to make that assessment. Trust your gut and continue to push if you feel there is an issue. You won't regret doing so. But you don't want to have to regret the time you waited too long or did nothing.

3 PUT ON YOUR OWN OXYGEN MASK

When Sophia was in the hospital, the last thing we thought about was ourselves. Our first-born precious baby was fighting for her life. We did not exercise. We didn't get good sleep. We ate whatever was in front of us, and it wasn't always very healthy. The idea of a hobby or personal time was out the door. Let's face it, some days I couldn't tell you whether we had a shower. Those ten weeks in the hospital were a blur. If you are nodding your head while reading this, it's because every parent I interviewed has been through some version of this part of their story.

That fight-or-flight mode can do wonders for you and for your child. Those parental instincts kicking in can give you strength you never imagined. But over time, that intense focus on everyone else can also drain you. It's a cruel irony that you put yourself last to be strong for them, but in doing so, you often weaken your ability to do just that.

When I spoke with parents, there was not a lot of middle-ground thought and opinions on this subject. Some suggested finding balance, embracing exercise, taking time out, and more. But those were the exceptions. Most reported they knew the importance of self-care but confessed they were just honestly not very good at it.

DON'T FALL FOR THE IRONY TRAP. SELF-CARE IS NOT SELFISH.

Being a parent to a child with a disability is like being in a club you never planned to join. There are a lot of paths into the club. Some learn in utero that their child will face challenges. For parents like LeAnn and me, Sophie's traumatic birth changed our lives forever. Many parents experience a typical birth but notice delays in the early years. And finally, some parents choose to adopt a child knowing full well their challenges.

> The paths and points of entry vary, but the emotional experiences are amazingly the same. And part of that journey includes a period where the entire world stops, and taking care of your child is your only focus.

It's natural to think our own needs do not matter. We will sleep at their bedside. Things like daily hygiene become optional. We either do not eat at all, or we abandon any discipline and eat like a teenager on a road trip. The stress of the times can also trigger some of our not-so-healthy relationships with food and cause us to overeat. Let's get real —while the world may be turned upside down, we know we have never been let down by a good slice of pizza or a Reese's peanut butter cup! Are you with me?

If we do break through and even consider doing something to take care of ourselves, we nip that instinct in the bud with a large serving of guilt. How dare we do something for us when our child needs us every minute of every day?

When you are in the heat of the battle, you lack perspective and abandon common sense. We all know what happens when we don't charge our cell phones. You've probably had a time when you should have pulled over but kept driving late into the night and almost had a wreck. Or how often have you snapped at someone during a stressful situation because you were tired, or worse yet, hangry?

You want to be there for your child. Their needs come first. I hear you and I get it. But you can't be there and be your best self if you are depleted. Read these words, and then say them out loud:

- I can't be there for my child if I am not strong.
- They *need me* right now, which means they need the *best* me—physically, emotionally, mentally strong.
- I must take care of myself so I *can* be there for them.

MENTAL HEALTH IS CRITICAL BUT OFTEN OVERLOOKED

Not long after Sophia came home from the hospital, we had several therapists come to our house each week. There is great care given to the needs of the child. But never once on that journey did anyone ask how we were doing. When you think of other situations like cancer, dementia, or even a family dealing with addiction, great care is given to the mental impact of the struggle for the patient as well as those around them.

If you have a child with a disability, you are no stranger to assessments. Our kids are being measured more than most. But never once did I hear of a parent who got an assessment of the toll this battle was taking on their mental health.

Start by finding an outlet to share what you are experiencing.

I have kept a journal for over thirty years, which has always been a place for me to process my feelings. Many parents suggested some type of counseling. Others leaned heavily into their faith. Many noted their biggest help came from talking to other parents whose children faced similar challenges. Being able to talk with people who get it and do not judge you can be a way to take care of yourself.

THEY WERE RIGHT; EXERCISE AND NUTRITION DO MATTER

Eating a balanced diet is important for everyone, but for parents of kids with disabilities, it has to do with energy. We've all had those times when we overindulged and then felt the downside of a sugar spike or just felt lethargic and lacking in energy. Parenting is a 24/7 gig in general. But throw in the extra daily routine of getting from point A to point B, which is the life of a special needs parent, and you need more energy. That's to say nothing of the energy it takes to constantly be the advocate for your child and push for what they need.

When you are making complex decisions—going to and from doctor visits, to school, and to therapy—you need all the energy you can muster. If you see food as your fuel, then you will likely be more selective. Your daily menu should be one that is full of whole foods, fruits, vegetables, lean meats, and things that have been proven to give you more energy. It's also an area where extra weight becomes a challenge physically and even in terms of your emotional state.

> Exercise is important for the health of all bodies. But if your child's disability has a physical side, it's not just important, but essential.

Although she wore a brace, Sophia has always been able to move on her own. But when your child uses a wheelchair or has limited mobility, the physical demands are greater. Being fit enables you to help lift and transfer your child. The cruel twist is that as they get older, they typically get heavier, adding to the physical demands of parenting. At the same time, they are harder to support because we are getting older, which for many presents a challenge to staying strong. This is why regular movement, weight training, and other proven forms of staying fit are going to help you respond to the physical demands of being a caregiver for your child.

Exercise can also provide needed alone time. When done with others it can take on a social aspect. Both are great, not just for your body, but for your emotional state. This is not an all-or-nothing concept. You don't need to become a triathlete. You just need to make movement part of your life to take care of your body.

SELF-CARE COMES IN ALL SHAPES AND SIZES

When most of us think of self-care, we imagine bubble baths or weekend getaways. The first key to taking care of yourself is to realize that self-care comes in many shapes and sizes. Refine self-care as anything that fuels you and allows you to recharge.

Here are some of the ideas I gathered from interviews.

- *Know your needs.* If you love music, then carving out ten minutes to listen to your favorite artist may quench your spirit. But if you prefer gaming, then fifteen minutes on the headset might do the trick.
- *Try a swap.* Many parents find others in the same boat. Arrange a day where you can take their kids along with yours, giving one parent time off and creating a built-in play date of sorts.
- *Find moments.* Respite doesn't have to be a day. Fifteen minutes to enjoy a warm cup of your favorite coffee while listening to music can be just what you need to power through the rest of your day.
- *Divide and conquer.* Take turns with your significant other with one watching the kids and the other doing anything they want during that window.
- *Wake up early.* Set the alarm so you can have fifteen to thirty minutes of solitary quiet time at the start of the day. It will feel like giving up sleep but add a sense of calm and start your day in the right frame of mind.

- *Don't overschedule.* It's a modern dynamic that we tend to stay so busy doing that we rarely have a chance to just be. Look at the planner of any parent, and you'll see it's easy to take on so much that life seems to be just about moving from appointment to appointment. Learning to say no creates space in the day for you and your child to not always feel like life is a race.

For most of us, I think the first time you get on a plane, it takes a minute to understand the whole oxygen-mask advice. Imagine sitting on a plane enjoying a trip with your elderly mother or your small child. Then suddenly, your stomach drops, and the plane starts to descend. Your mind races, and your chest pounds. Of course, your gut instinct is going to be to rush to their aid. But you can't do them much good if you have passed out. Imagine them struggling for air and wishing you could help them. Meanwhile, you are slumped over in your seat. It's an extreme example, but the point is, in that moment, you need to get secure so you can be there for others.

Raising a child with a disability can feel like that same stomach drop every single day. If you don't secure yourself, your ability to do the one thing you desire most—be there for your child—will be compromised.

TAKE CARE OF YOURSELF

For Crimson Claycomb, life as a mother to three kids—one with very involved medical needs—was an endless list of tasks. Time to wake up the kids. Time to get everyone ready. Time to go to the doctors, the ball games, the activities. Time to make dinner early and bring it to-go so the kids could grab a bite between one activity and the other. "It felt like I was constantly chasing a string of confetti inside a tornado."

With seizures and constant medical episodes, life was an endless string of "drop everything and go" events that left her constantly tending to the needs of everyone in the house—except her own. "It's not that my needs were low on the list. I was not even *on* the list." She lost weight, felt rundown, and was low on energy. "It was hard for me to muster the energy to walk through the grocery store. I disconnected from people and isolated myself. I truly understand how people can get to a place where they see suicide as the best way out of their situation."

She quickly realized that the day-to-day challenges of special needs parenting were taking a physical and mental toll on her that was impacting everyone in the house. It became a vicious cycle. By putting everyone else first, she became run-down, which made her less able to help her family. She knew that to make a change, she had to let go of a lot of negative beliefs about herself and about being a mother. "I had to learn that I had a right to feel loved, a right to feel secure, and a right to be happy. I had to let go of the idea that you are a bad mom if you feel like you need a short break from your own kids."

Crimson knew that in order to be at her best, she had to take care of herself first. "Things changed when I realized I needed to be a leader in my house. My kids were watching me and learning from me. It matters what I do when I get angry. It matters what I cook and how I eat. It matters what type of mood I wake up in, because that sets the tone for the day with my family." She also had to let go of caring what others think. "I think, in part, I did so much because I was worried about how people would see me as a mom. But I realized what mattered was my happiness and my kids' happiness."

The good news is, Crimson has made big changes that have impacted everyone in the family. "Today, I am in such a better place. The confetti is still there. But I feel like it's inside a lava lamp, and it is contained. I don't let it dictate my life. We still have crazy events, but I realize they don't have to take over our entire lives." She had to learn to ask for help, to set boundaries, and to say no. She also had to find ways to step away and tend to her own mental and emotional health. "Today, self-care is promoted and expected. It is possible to change your mindset. Trust me, if I can do it, anyone can."

4 IT TAKES A VILLAGE

Before we were allowed to leave the hospital, Sophia had to pass the "car seat challenge." This involved sitting in her car seat while still using oxygen for a period of time without her oxygen saturation levels (sats) dropping. We sat in the room as each tick of the clock seemed to take a lifetime. It felt a bit like a family on the sidelines of a track meet. We held our breath and waited. Then a smile and sense of relief came over us because, after ten grueling weeks, Sophia was coming home—and it even happened to be on Mother's Day!

Most first-time parents will confess to you that when they first got their baby home, amid the joy they also felt a bit of panic and emotional overload. They find themselves thinking, "Okay. What do we do *now*?" For us, that typical feeling was multiplied because Sophia was just over three pounds, still on oxygen, and the road ahead for all of us was anything but clear. We were an emotional mix of relieved, excited, and terrified. We knew we needed help on this new path. We had to build our "village" and surround our family with people and experiences to help Sophia thrive.

BE CAREFUL NOT TO ISOLATE

When Sophia came home, she was so fragile we were very protective about the number of people she could be around for fear of infections like RSV or pneumonia. We did not have many people over and did not really leave the house for most of her first year. It made us a bit stir-crazy, and at times our only relief was to drive around in the car. I remember one instance where one of us stayed in the car with Sophia just so the other person could walk around Target. For a bit, this was our grasp on sanity. When you are spending so much time taking care of your young child, many parents run the risk of becoming isolated from their friends and family at a time when they need them the most.

While some of it is logistics and fear of infection, there are also emotional aspects at play. It's common to feel like nobody else knows exactly what you are going through. You often find yourself feeling such worry, anxiety, fear, guilt, and a general sense of overload that you are not quite ready to be around others, let alone to share your feelings with everyone you know. Be careful not to shut others out and withdraw.

CONNECT WITH OTHERS IN YOUR SHOES

Find other parents who have been in your shoes. This is where the internet, from Facebook groups to moms on TikTok, is a modern-day godsend. You can also turn to nonprofits in your area who often have parent education and support as a major part of their mission. In some cases, organizations have a sort of "welcome wagon" that even comes to the hospital and reaches out to comfort new parents.

When talking to other parents, you will get a sense of community knowing you are not alone, you are not crazy, and others get it and have felt the exact range of emotions you have. Feeling like you now are part of that pack is a game-changer. You also can let your guard down with this group because there is a lack of judgment. You feel an instant kinship because they get it and have felt what you are feeling. It's a great way to calm your fears when you hear that they faced similar struggles, pushed through, and today are doing well. There is nothing more soothing than to hear that their teenager, while still facing challenges, is living a full and joyous life. This sense of connection will have you feeling less alone and more hopeful about your child's future.

> When you can let go of some of that worry, you can focus on the path ahead, even though it likely still looks rocky.

Often you still feel a little lost. Imagine going on a vacation to Europe. You bring a few guidebooks but still need to figure out all the details for yourself. When do the trains run? Which day is the museum closed? Where can I get the best meal? Now compare that to arriving in a new city with a local tour guide who was born and raised there. Suddenly you know where to eat, where to shop. Not only do you know where to go, but the tour guide also gives you the inside scoop on what to avoid.

Fellow parents can help you navigate early things like doctor visits, ways to incorporate therapy into your daily routine, financial resources, and more. Today, there are groups out there for just about anything. One mom shared how relieved and validated she was when she found other moms whose kids only ate a few items. "You think you are the only one. And your friends or family give you advice based on their kids, which is not the same. There is an instant bond when you find another parent who sees you and truly gets you because they have been in your shoes." Surrounding yourself with other parents who are on a similar path will be a key to your journey.

GET YOUR CHILD INVOLVED IN ACTIVITIES

For kids with cerebral palsy (CP), the tone in their muscles is often affected. Sophia's CP was on her left side. She would tend to walk up on her toes. To correct this, she wore an ankle foot orthotic (AFO) which is basically a brace that ran from her foot to her knee. Because of her vision issues, she wore thick glasses and often had a patch on one eye. For kids with disabilities, it can feel like everywhere you go, the first thing the world sees is how you are different. This is why getting your child involved in doing something they enjoy has so many benefits.

Sometimes you will want to do activities that are adaptive in a more segmented community where everybody doing the activity also has a disability. Today, we are lucky that more opportunities exist than ever, from Special Olympics to sled hockey to social skills groups at some therapy centers. Sophia was involved in a fashion show at the Kids Center where she got therapy. These activities provide a place where your child sees others like them. It's also a chance for your child to be the star, the one in the spotlight.

Being involved with an adaptive sport or activity can help you bring a sense of normalcy to your life.

They will also more easily make friends, perhaps because the barrier of being different is removed in these settings. During my interviews, I heard countless stories of kids who met at a very young age doing an adaptive activity and grew up with that group of kids. Kids will also learn the value of hard work and practice, how to work in a team, and how to listen to a coach. As parents, you will benefit because while your kids are busy having fun, you will be on the stands or the sidelines with fellow parents. Just like any "soccer mom" or "volleyball dad," you will soon form a social bond with these parents. In some cases, you will focus on this journey and share practical ideas and tips for navigating daily life. In other cases, your connection will be about raising money for the team, preparing potluck dinners, or getting ready for a team road trip—just like parents of typically abled athletes.

Most parents I talked with also got their child involved in nonadaptive experiences so they could integrate with other kids whenever possible. Sophia did gymnastics. Looking back, this was kind of amazing because her CP made her muscles very tight, and she could not stretch or do things others could do. When she was young, she would trip and fall a lot because of her brace, vision, and sense of balance. Early on, during a tumbling class, the physical struggle to do the activities made her have a meltdown. She had lost it, and I felt the glares of other parents. Let's just say we could not get to the parking lot fast enough. But she was still drawn to it, so we went back, and eventually, we found a gym she could call home.

Gymnastics can be intense and give kids a sense of pressure that risks taking out the fun. Although it took her longer to master every move, she kept fighting and pushing herself. Physically, it was great for her body, like sneaking in more physical therapy. Mentally, it was teaching her resilience and other lessons that come from things like sports. This also expanded her social circle outside of school and her friends from the Kids Center.

Every child with a disability's path is different. Remember, they are still kids who laugh at fart jokes, need to burn off energy, have tender emotions, and have dreams. If you look into the room of just about every little girl, you are going to find a pair of ruby or glass slippers. It doesn't matter if you also find a brace, a walker, or wheelchair; all kids have things they love and activities that will help them grow. Also remember that your child is not their disability. It is a part of them, but they are not a blank slate for us as parents to mold. Their spirit, their fight, and their determination will go a long way to determining their future.

CONNECT WITH ORGANIZATIONS

For just about every diagnosis, there are nonprofits dedicated to supporting families facing that challenge. Think of nonprofits as a bit of a "superstore" or "one-stop shop" for building your village. They can give you access to quality and vetted information that will help you become educated on your child's diagnosis. They can connect you to other parents who are facing similar issues or who have in the past. They are usually aware of medical providers in your community who work with your type of need and can even give advice on how to navigate the world of medicine. They often offer therapy services that can directly impact your child. Many offer adapted activities from the arts, sports, and more. Most offer social outings for kids and families. Some nonprofits offer things like a summer camp for kids and/or families. Nonprofits can also offer parent support, often in the form of respite activities or even support groups.*

THE VILLAGE STARTS AT HOME

Ironically, your family and friends, those closest to you, can be a source of challenge and conflict. I will call this group your network. But if you learn how to navigate this part of the journey, they can be your greatest resource.

When Sophia was born, we had so many people wrap their arms around us. We had hospital visits, cards, donations of gift cards, and more. We didn't have a nursery ready, so my friend Mary from work came over and even helped us strip old wallpaper so we could quickly paint Sophia's room. Your family, friends, coworkers, church group... They all want to help you. But figuring out exactly what to do with your network can actually *add* stress.

Part of the challenge comes down to logistics. What exactly can others do to help, and how can we avoid creating more work by trying to manage and communicate with them? The other part comes down to our willingness to ask for help and to take it. We tend to want to put on a brave face and tell the world everything is fine. But you will need help. Are you willing to ask for it? Are you willing to take it?

One mom said she had to take off her "superwoman" cape long enough to admit she needed help. When she finally gave in, she broke down in tears and asked her best friend to just come over and mop her kitchen floor. It's okay to let your network in to help you.

---

* Tune into the Seeing Ability Podcast for continued insights from nonprofits working in this field.

I have to say we were blessed with a hundred percent support from our families. When my parents would visit, we would sometimes find my dad missing for hours. Later, we learned he had snuck out to visit Sophia, where he would sit by her incubator for hours. He bought a small tape player and recorded his voice so they could play it over and over for her when he was gone. My parents lived in Florida, and I will never forget our visit when Sophia was about two, and they had a party so all of their Florida friends could finally meet this "miracle baby" they had prayed about together. We were blessed with an abundance of help and a lack of conflict with our families.

Family and friends can also represent a potential pitfall on the journey, which most are not able to avoid.

This has to do with how others show up for you compared to what you expected from them. You are most likely going to find yourself feeling totally abandoned and let down by some of your family, friends, and coworkers you thought would be your rocks. Others will seem to move on with their regular life and typical kids and not go out of their way to include you. Trust me, this can be one of the most painful parts of your early life as a special needs parent. This will hurt and will probably make you angry. Prepare yourself for this, and realize it will be hard.

Find a way to get past these feelings, give a lot of grace, and realize there are a variety of reasons why people may not be able to show up the way you want them to. In the end, find a way to let go of the people who are not in your life, and appreciate the people who are. Meet people where they are, accept what they can give, and let go of how you expected them to react.

Like many parts of the journey, reading this chapter won't give you a pass on this pain, but it might help you not be surprised by it and allow you to move on faster. You don't have to cut off people who let you down. They are still part of your community and still care about you and your child. They may show up later, and you will be glad you did not cut ties with them.

It can be helpful to proactively brainstorm a list of ways people can help. You can also take inventory of the skills of your network.

- We all have that aunt who loves to plan family reunions and trips. They can become your volunteer coordinator.
- If you have someone with a medical background, they could go with you to doctor visits.
- Maybe you have someone who is great at research and can help you learn about the diagnosis.
- There is always someone great with kids who might be able to give you respite or help watch your other children.
- For a full list of creative ideas I gathered from families, see Appendix 2.

Once you move through acceptance and get ready to move forward on the new path, you have to build a team around your child and your family. Avoid the pitfall of isolation by connecting to other families who have faced similar battles. Find activities your child enjoys, and your community will continue to grow. Connect with nonprofits and organizations working with your particular set of diagnoses or challenges. And enlist the home team: your friends and family. You will end up feeling less alone, and you will have a variety of people on your side to help you and your child thrive.

CREATING HER OWN VILLAGE TURNED INTO HELPING OTHERS

When Samantha Fields and her husband Jorome got a diagnosis of autism for their son Trayson, they felt lost at what to do next or where to turn. He started to get therapy at a local center, and that got them talking with therapists about resources. Each week, they found themselves in the lobby with other parents on a similar path. "While our situations were all different, I was surprised by how common our challenges were as parents," explained Samantha. "It was good to be around others who knew what we were going through."

Navigating family and friends was challenging for the Fields. "You discover really fast who is going to be there for you and who is not," Samantha added. When Trayson was invited to a typical birthday party, they had to decline because they knew the noise and chaos of the party would cause a sensory meltdown for Trayson. The hosts of such parties often got offended and did not realize the challenges for Samantha and her son.

Over time, some friends came around and gained new insights, while other friends just needed to be let go.

They also faced some unique challenges with both sides of their family. "With one group, we got a bit of denial because due to their strong faith, they felt we could just pray it away. With the other side, we got a lot of judgment around our parenting choices." One day, Trayson was outside when a neighbor fired up a chainsaw. Samantha immediately ran to get his headphones to help him calm his senses. Immediately, Trayson's relative said he did not need those things and accused her of "babying" her son.

They also faced challenges with people respecting their choices. Trayson eats a specific diet that helps him regulate. But when he would visit houses of relatives, they tossed out those rules. "They thought we were just not being fun or being too strict instead of learning why what we were doing was actually critical for him," Samantha explained.

With so many differences among family and friends, Samantha got an idea. She figured she wasn't the only parent who felt isolated or struggled to have family and friends respect and understand her needs and those of her son. What she needed was a community that got it. She made a social media post to see if people felt there was a need for a group to hold sensory-friendly events and act as a support group for parents. Immediately, she was flooded with replies. She even got an offer of free space for the group to have events and activities. Parents wanted a space where their kids would not be judged and where they could meet other parents in the same boat.

She decided to formally start a 501(c)(3) nonprofit. "The name was kind of related to Trayson. We always joked it was his world, and we were just living in it," added Samantha. They formally named their nonprofit A Different World. In their first year, the group hosted at least one event per month. Parents flocked to the group. Sometimes to have your village, you might need to be the one to create it. Learn more about A Different World by visiting adwinc.org.

5 DEALING WITH OTHERS

With her constant stumbles, her leg brace, and a patch over her left eye, Sophia got her fair share of looks everywhere we went with her. It doesn't matter if your child uses a walker, rolls into every room in a wheelchair, or has facial anomalies that make them appear different, going into the world with your child who has a disability is going to be noticed. Be prepared for people to stop and stare as if you were an alien or an attraction at the circus. Also be prepared for people to ask questions. What may start as a shock and annoyance, however, can turn into an opportunity to build bridges if you're up for it.

There will also be plenty of questions and comments, often from total strangers who do not know you or your child. Some are predictable and understandable, especially if you think back to how little most of us knew about the world of disability before having our kids. But others will take you back. One mom shared how a total stranger asked her, "What is his life expectancy going to be?" When Sophie was little, a woman at the store joked with us, "What did you do to her leg, dad?" And some comments will just be plain hurtful, like a parent I interviewed who had a person at the mall turn to her husband and say, "She should not even bring him out in public."

TAKE STOCK OF YOUR INITIAL REACTION

There is no way to control the stares, questions, or actions of others. And it's totally normal for this to bring up a lot of feelings for you at first. When Sophia was young, we would feel self-conscious and even a bit embarrassed. You may feel angry. You might feel frustrated and annoyed with others. You could even feel sad or discouraged that on top of navigating the challenges of your child's disability, you now have to deal with the questions and reactions of others. Start by acknowledging how you feel. Resist the temptation to deny your feelings or feel guilty for even having this type of reaction. It's natural and part of the process.

CONSIDER THE OPPORTUNITY

Once you've taken stock of how you feel, you get to choose how you react. This takes practice and intention. In the beginning, you might not react at all, or you might snap back. But most people I spoke with said they eventually learned to see the questions and stares as an opportunity to educate and help others feel more comfortable around people who are different.

Some parents told me it helped them to write responses and to develop a sort of script for common questions. Others saw questions as a chance to draw people in and start a conversation.

Try breaking the ice and acknowledging the adult or child asking seems to have questions, and encourage it. This typically changes the tone and attitude of the person you are talking with. Another idea is to build a bridge by noting a commonality between your child and the person asking the question. For example, if a child asks, "Why can't she walk?" you might answer, "She has a medical issue that makes her leg not work like yours or mine. I see you like Ninja Turtles; so does she. Who is your favorite turtle?" This approach lets others see that your child is just a kid, and while they may be different, they are more like other children than different. We all have things we can't do. The kid asking the question may be a terrible singer or is not very good at sports. The difference is they don't wear a T-shirt that says, "My voice makes dogs howl in pain."

Encourage questions. You will likely have a child ask a question, but their parent may shush them or scold them for being rude. Let the child and parent know it's natural to be curious, it's okay for them to ask, and you'd love to talk to them and answer their questions. This teaches both the child and the parent that talking with a kid with a disability and their families is not off-limits. It also again shows them you have more in common with them than you have differences.

MODEL HOW YOU WANT YOUR CHILD TO REACT

Another reason to be purposeful about how you handle the questions and stares is because your child is watching you. We are our child's first teacher, and that truth is not limited to schoolwork. We model for them how we handle stress. And when a person asks a seemingly awkward or intrusive question, this is a chance to teach our kids how to be graceful, to be that ambassador, and to build bridges. If your child sees you get angry and frustrated, that is likely how they will react. On the other hand, if they see you be friendly, upbeat, and notice how you draw people in and engage them in conversation, they will be more likely to do the same.

HIDDEN CAN BE HARDER

It is important to note that a hidden disability can be more challenging. If your child uses a wheelchair or walker, most people will know they have a disability and provide them a bit of space and grace. But if your child looks typical on the outside but has meltdowns or other behaviors tied to their diagnosis, this can make things way harder. You are likely to not only get the stares and looks, but also a hearty dose of judgment from other parents about how you are raising your child.

You might be tempted to get angry, want to scream, or want to put the other person in their place. This is totally natural and very real. Not only is your child being treated like some type of sideshow, but now they are calling into question you as a parent. This is where patience, grace, taking stock of your emotions, and being intentional about your response is even more key.

Most parents told me in this situation, they chose to just ignore others and move on about their business. Some found graceful ways to educate others, resisting the temptation to throw it back in their face, and instead building bridges and increasing understanding.

KEEP PRIVACY IN MIND

Many parents reported their response to stares and questions changed over time, especially when they started to consider the privacy of their child. I will never forget a story one mom told me about a discussion at work about her grandson's disability. After sharing what she was going through, a coworker shared how her twenty-eight-year-old nephew had a disability that made him not only impotent but also incontinent. The details of her nephew's condition were told to her in private and were not meant to be shared. It was not her story to tell. You do not owe every person you interact with a full medical history of your child. Remember, it's not your medical history, it's theirs.

It's also important to teach your child it's okay for them to claim boundaries. Their disability or medical condition is their own private information. They do not owe an explanation of their disability to every person they meet.

When your kid wears braces, uses a wheelchair, or acts differently, the world is going to notice. While most people, young and old, are going to have innocent questions, there are always going to be a few jerks out there who are mean or rude to you or your child. This always has way more to do with them than with you. You will realize over time it's natural for others to have questions, and it's also natural for you to get annoyed or angry when they ask them. Both can be true at the same time. However, if you can work through your initial emotions and get to a place where you not only tolerate but even welcome these situations, it will be better for you. You will find yourself being an educator and building bridges, and you will be showing your child the right way to navigate the outside world as a person with a disability.

A STRANGER GIVES THE SHIRT OFF HIS BACK

Not every interaction with the world is a negative one. There are times when others will step up and surprise you with kindness, an open heart, total acceptance, and love.

Jake Lapekas and his parents are *big* Disney fans. When they got off the Main Street train at Walt Disney World, Jake noticed a couple in front of him, and the man was wearing a "party shirt" with *Cars 2* characters all over it. His mom, Kathleen, stopped the couple to ask about the shirt, since they had been searching all over for just such an item for Jake, age twelve, who was an enormous *Cars* fan. As his mom started to talk, Jake wrapped his arm around the man's arm and gave him an enormous smile. His mother started to apologize and explain how Jake's autism caused him sometimes to not recognize typical boundaries. But the man just looked down at Jake and smiled, telling the family that they needed to talk to "the war department," which was his wife, about the origins of his shirt. They discovered that the shirt had been purchased online before the trip.

The man, so touched by Jake's sweet admiration, surprised everyone by taking off his shirt (he had on a T-shirt underneath) and insisting that Jake have it. The parents protested, but the man simply said, "This is a great kid, and you would truly honor me if you would accept this for him."

The shirt was a few sizes too big but has fit better as Jake has gotten older. He wears his special shirt only on days when the family goes to church. It is a reminder to them about the time they stumbled on true kindness and generosity from a man they will never know but will also never forget.

6 FAMILY IMPACT

I will never forget watching Sophia the day our son Peter was born. There she sat, wearing a summer dress with white pearls. Her eyes lit up behind her thick round glasses. As she held Peter in her arms, you could see about five bracelets on her wrist. (That girl loves to accessorize!) She was very excited about this little person who had been added to our lives. But little did Peter know that for a big part of his young life, he was going to be the "plus one" for Sophia's therapy sessions, doctor appointments, and surgeries.

There is no denying that having a child with a disability in your household packs your schedule and has the potential of becoming the center of everything you do. While the circumstances are somewhat unavoidable, how you navigate that dynamic is up to you.

RECOGNIZE THE IMPACT ON SIBLINGS

Having a child with a disability is going to impact their siblings. Sophia was the first grandchild on both sides of our family. And because she came over three months early, she quickly became the center of the universe for six grandparents. I am not sure her feet ever touched the ground when they were around. In those early years, our lives were very hectic, and our calendars were very full with multiple therapy trips, a daily home therapy routine, and Sophia just taking a little more time to navigate the world around her.

Do not get me wrong, Peter got love and affection too. But I think because he could reach all those physical and developmental milestones so effortlessly, it was sort of assumed he would be fine, while Sophie needed extra support at each step along the way.

I will never forget a story one mom told me that crystalizes how this journey can impact a sibling. She took her kids to see Santa, and to her surprise, the sibling asked Santa if she could get spina bifida for Christmas. Why would she ask to get a disability? In her eyes, having spina bifida—like her sister—meant you got to go on trips with just you, Mom, and Dad. It also meant getting stuffed animals from time to time. Of course, the younger daughter didn't realize that special time and toys meant painful surgeries followed by long recovery. But it gave that mom a wake-up call that she needed to consider how their journey was impacting everyone.

> Take a moment to step back and realize your other kids are going to have less of your time.

It's also not about a tally of minutes, but also about where you focus your energy and attention. Being aware of this; trying to give your other kids what they need is vital. Below are some of the ways you can do this.

TALK ABOUT THE ELEPHANT

It's important to talk to your other kids as early as possible about the elephant in the room—being a brother or sister to someone with a disability. Siblings want to know you care about how they feel. They also want to feel like you understand having a brother or sister with a disability has an impact on them. Talk to them about what it's like.

Give them a safe space to communicate their frustrations. Find out if they feel like they are missing out on certain things or not getting attention from you. Not only will you be better able to meet their needs, but you will also be teaching them how to tackle difficult topics in an open and honest way. Being heard and knowing you are thinking about how they feel is a big piece of the puzzle.

MAKE TIME FOR EACH CHILD

It's easy to feel like everything in your life, and in this case your family, is related to raising a child with a disability. But the challenge of quality time with each kid is a very real thing for any house with multiple children. Most parents I talked with said they made sure to carve out time for each of their children.

In some cases, this means a night out with Mom. In others, it means a grandparent babysitting so both parents can have a special time with each of their children. Many parents divide and conquer, so one parent gets that carved-out special time with just one child, while the other parent holds down the fort. One couple recalled a story of how some people at their church told them how much they admired how friendly they were as a divorced couple. They laughed and had to let people know they were not in fact divorced, but just had split duties and alternated weeks so everyone could have a good experience.

> While separate and special time is key, it does not have to come down to a math formula.

This is more about understanding what is important to each child and trying to give them what they need. One mom shared her philosophy with her children was, "Everyone gets what they need. But that does not always mean everyone is going to get the same."

GIVE THEM THE OPPORTUNITY TO BECOME AN ADVOCATE

You don't want your other kids to feel like it's their job to raise your child with special needs. That said, involve them in their care, and let them be a part of their sibling's routine if possible. One occupational therapist recommended a simulation where you try to have your other kids experience what it must be like to go through the world as a person with a disability. This can create a sense of empathy and open the door to conversations about feelings.

Most parents said the fiercest defenders of their child with special needs were the siblings. If anyone in the family had the risk of flying off the handle at a stare or a question, it was going to be the brother or sister. One benefit for siblings is growing up learning to be more tolerant and accepting of people who are different, which can be very valuable to them as adults. In fact, several parents said one of their other kids chose to go into a field like teaching or therapy because they enjoyed helping to take care of their sibling.

LET GO OF PERFECTION

It's tempting to want to make your experience like any other family. But this might be unrealistic. One mom shared a story about how trying to plan the perfect outing that included everyone made things worse for her and everyone in the family. Her younger daughter wanted to see *Disney on Ice* with her cousins. The mom also wanted to bring her other daughter who used a chair. The logistical challenges of requesting accessible seating, having enough seats for everyone, and managing potty breaks, snack runs, and so on made the entire night stressful and less fun for the whole family.

She realized it would have been way more enjoyable to take her child with special needs one night and arrange to have the rest of the group go another time. She also discovered what really mattered was the time they spent as family not during these big events, but during the daily things like having dinner or watching a movie together.

The pressure to make those perfect family moments may not be worth it. But the true family moments are the little ones that happen every day.

TAKE CARE AS A COUPLE

I love being a dad and have yet to meet another parent who would trade parenting for anything. Being there to help my kids go from helpless babies to thriving adults has been exhilarating, humbling, scary, and downright exhausting at times. But the foundation of each of our parenting experiences is the partnership that exists in the home. Few couples take the time along the journey of raising their child with a disability to consider the pressures this particular journey has on their relationship—good and bad.

> Just like self-care is key for you to be a good parent, tending to your relationship as a couple is essential if you are going to support your child and yourselves in the process.

I have been blessed in this area. After twenty-six years of marriage, I still get excited every time I hear LeAnn's voice on the phone. I am a crazy romantic, and luckily she puts up with me. That is not to say that we haven't faced challenges. First, we had a micro-preemie born at just twenty-six weeks, one and a half pounds, with lots of complications and years of therapy, surgery, and stress.

Then, over twenty years ago, LeAnn was diagnosed with breast cancer. We got the official news on a trip of a lifetime. My mother had always wanted to see the Macy's Day Parade in New York City. There we were, in the midst of this "bucket list" experience in a hotel room overlooking the parade route, when we got the call that the biopsy results were positive and LeAnn would need to have an aggressive double mastectomy to fight cancer. Once again, the world was in slow motion, and we were back in the center of another storm.

These types of external battles can strengthen or crush a relationship. I am blessed to say they have strengthened ours. What follows is my best collection of advice taken from my own experience, my interviews for this book, and reading on the subject.

Put Your Relationship First.

It's natural to think of everyone else. But the foundation of being parents in the first place is the love that brought you together. You don't need to go far to see the stats that relationships are hard for everyone. But add in the emotions of this new path, and it's a possible recipe for disaster if you are not proactive. While both of you are ready at any minute to fight for your child, be just as committed to fight and protect your relationship. As one parent put it, "If Mom and Dad are alright, the kids will be alright."

A Healthy Relationship Starts with Communication.

Hands down, having open and honest communication was the biggest advice I heard on this topic. If you were good communicators before this child arrived, rely on those skills. This does not mean just being in the loop and knowing what is going on that day.

> Communicate how you feel, your highs, your lows, your frustrations—even if those are sometimes with each other.

Consider journaling and then sharing what you wrote with each other to get all those feelings out. Understand what each of you are feeling. What's the true fear you don't want anyone else to know? How do you feel you are failing as a parent or as a partner that you are afraid to say out loud? Do you have guilt? Are you feeling sad or depressed? Are you having trouble being motivated? Do you worry if you have what it takes to do this but are afraid to admit that to your partner? This is a time for "all the feels," as they say. You have to create an environment where you feel like you can share the good and the bad. This is especially true of the bad. Establish a safe space where you do not feel judged for admitting how you truly feel.

Let Your Partner Know Your Needs and Work to Discover Theirs.

When you are venting about your child's doctor's appointment, are you wanting your partner to offer a solution, or do you just need someone to listen and validate how you are feeling? When you come to bed after an exhausting day, do you want them to step up and offer more help, or are you just looking for a little appreciation and acknowledgment of your hard work? Often, parents discovered their partner really didn't know their needs, yet they also admitted they were not very good at sharing what those were in the first place.

Try to communicate your needs, but also ask yourself if you are offering your partner what they need most.

This lack of judgment leads me to another major piece of advice: Give each other a great deal of grace and forgiveness. We all make mistakes. Sometimes when we are under pressure, we do not show up as our best selves. Ask any set of older parents with grown kids, and they will tell you parenting is the most rewarding job they've ever had but also at times the most challenging, humbling, and frustrating one. The couples I talked with recommended letting your partner know you have their back even when they mess up. Let them know you love them unconditionally, even when they are angry, grumpy, sad, or just difficult to be around. Grace and forgiveness are two ingredients that help you ride the ups and downs you will face on this journey.

But what do you do if that type of open and honest communication has never been your thing? Many couples know they should share openly but just don't feel they have the skills to do so. This might be a good time to work with a counselor, someone in your faith community, mentor, or other help. It might take an outside, objective person to help you open up. Too often people only turn to that outside help when things are bad and you are working to save your relationship. My advice is to start that early, while you are in the center of the storm, to take a more proactive approach to head off problems before they arise.

Remind Yourselves of Why You are Together in the First Place.

In the early years of navigating this new path, you are in the center of a pretty big storm that neither one of you signed up for. It's a lot. It's easy to forget your love for each other produced this child and landed you here in the first place. Stop and think about that. Your amazing child is on this earth because the two of you found each other. It's so easy with the daily grind to forget what a miracle your child is and the miracle of the love you share that brought them into this world. Stop and reflect on that. And a bond you both share is your unconditional love for that child and your desire for them to have the best life possible.

Carve Out Time As a Couple.

Like self-care, this can seem impossible. But it does not need to be an all-or-nothing scenario. Few parents in the heat of the special needs journey are going to get a weekend away on a tropical island. But leaning on your village so you can have regular date nights can be a lifeline to keeping your relationship healthy and front-and-center in your lives. Don't be afraid to ask for help.

There are a lot of things that can press on your relationship, from worrying to finances. But one of the biggest things is logistics and the day-to-day workload of this path. Luckily, most parents have a community of family and friends who see your struggle and want to help. Be able and willing to not only ask for their help but get creative as to what they can do for you. For a reminder of what you can ask others to do, check out Appendix 2 which we introduced in the village chapter. Any task you offload can reduce your stress and therefore take pressure off your relationship.

Share the Load.

Many parents reported a big source of their problems was an imbalance in various aspects of the work that needs to get done. A good example would be research. If one parent is the one reading the books, discussing in the parent groups, and so on, this can present a problem. The person who is not carrying the load feels detached and excluded, and the person doing all the work feels resentment that the burden is on their shoulders. This does not mean that every arena must be split fifty-fifty in terms of the hours or the workload. What it does mean is that the mental ownership of each aspect has to be shared and jointly owned. It can be easier to do a certain aspect yourself. But when you do, you run the risk of alienating your partner and burning yourself out. Take inventory of each of your strengths and tackle the journey by letting each of you take the lead in areas that match your strengths. If you avoid conflict like the plague, dealing with insurance carriers might not be your thing. That said, if your office files are the model of Zen, you might be the one to create a filing system that ties medical bills to EOBs. Play to each other's strengths, but make sure both people feel included even if they are not the lead worker bee in that area.

Take Some Time for Your Relationship Every Day.

One easy suggestion was to establish a great bedtime ritual. Good sleep is always important, so try to set a regular bedtime. Do something you enjoy, like reading or streaming a favorite TV show. Many couples use the time before bed as a time for "pillow talk" to wrap up and decompress from the day. It can be a good idea to establish a time when you will shut down screens and technology. Make sure time for intimacy is not forgotten either.

Give Each Person a Total Break from Their Duties.

This relates back to self-care. But it's the couple realizing they both need a break and making it a priority to give it. Whether it's Mom's night out with her best girlfriend or just Mom being able to be alone in another part of the house to read a book and not be doing "mom things" for a few moments, it's important. This total break, being "off the clock" entirely, was a repeated theme to allow parents to relax, to breathe, and to reset so they can come back refreshed and ready for battle. Couples who made it a priority to do this regularly found they were happier together and more able to be present for their child.

SISTER SEES THE WORLD DIFFERENTLY

A lot of people ask Georgia Payne what it's like having a sibling with a disability. In Georgia's case, she knows doubly how that is because her younger brother has autism, and her older brother has autism and spina bifida. "It's definitely different. I'd say it has good parts and bad parts. But the good parts are what I think of most."

Part of growing up is learning how to deal with stress and handle what life throws at you. Georgia's brother Nate has a lot of medical issues related to his spina bifida. When a medical crisis occurred, Georgia learned to spring into action along with her parents. "When it was something typical—like a broken bone—I was the one getting the supplies and keeping everyone calm. Then when it was something big, like a surgery, I would help too. One time when my brother went to surgery, I made him a basket of items I knew he'd enjoy when he came home." Learning to step up in a crisis made her grow up fast, stay calm and collected during a crisis, and be better equipped to handle problems that life throws at her.

Georgia said the downside of quickly maturing was sometimes wanting to just be a kid with fewer worries or problems—one whose only concern was playing with friends. There were also times when she felt less willing to share or vent about her problems because they paled in comparison to her siblings'. "I think I sometimes kept my problems inside more than would have been healthy. They were big things for a teenage girl. But compared to my brothers, it seemed kind of silly for me to complain about them."

Georgia tells parents not to get too worried that raising a child with special needs is going to damage the other kids. "Sure, you are going to spend more time with them. That just is part of the deal. But we understand." She did commend her mom for making sure they had one-on-one time to go shopping or out for food, no matter how busy family life was. "Your kid won't really mind the craziness of your life because that is normal to them. They don't know what normal is supposed to look like. So just make the experience good for them, and they will enjoy your version of normal."

She credits her sibling experience for shaping the way she sees the world. "I learned a lot of empathy. I don't judge people with a disability. I just see them as people. I don't set limits on what I think they can do." She wants to be a lawyer when she grows up, a choice that was also shaped by the journey. "I saw that people with disabilities need advocates. I think I want to be a lawyer because I want to help people."

7 SETTING THE BAR

When Sophia was born, the entire family rallied around her. When you are the first grandchild on both sides, you are going to get a lot of attention. But when you come into the world at one and a half pounds and everyone is praying for you to live, then you are going to maintain a special place in the hearts of aunts, uncles, grandparents, and of course, Mom and Dad. This was of course true for us, as we all celebrated and watched Sophia's every move in those early years. Raising any kid, parents balance the need to protect their kids with the need to let their child stretch and learn through experience. Finding the right balance can be especially challenging for parents of kids with any type of challenge or disability.

DITCH THE BUBBLE WRAP

Having a child with a disability intensifies the connection parents and family feel toward the journey of that child. But that level of attention and affection can also lead to a temptation to overprotect your child because you don't want them to go through any more pain or suffering.

It's a natural instinct. They've been through surgeries. They struggle with things other kids do with ease. You want to do anything you can to make life easier for them since they already struggle enough. But by doing too much for your child, you might be robbing them of the ability to learn how to become independent and do things for themselves.

> Many parents said they caught themselves doing too much in their child's early years.

One mom, whose son has spina bifida, said it hit her when she realized her son was just learning to self-catheterize at age twelve, while other families they know had their child doing this by age five. I spoke with a camp counselor who worked with a girl who blossomed one summer once her parents, who tended to do everything for her, left.

A shift happened around this issue when parents contemplated the long haul. If the goal is to raise an independent adult, doing things for them robs them of learning the skills they will one day need to live on their own. Also, by doing too much, you will miss out on being able to see your child achieve new things. Ask yourself who will do things for your child when you the parent are no longer around. Once you come to this realization, you will need to train Grandma, Grandpa, and the rest of the family to let go and give your child room to develop on their own. You want to be nearby to catch them if they fall. But you also want to let them fall and learn to get back up.

BE CAREFUL OF COMPARISON

I will never forget talking with our pediatrician about where Sophia stood on the growth charts. I think when she was little, she was in the second percentile, meaning out of one hundred kids her age, she was smaller than ninety-eight percent of them! For the next ten years, her grandmother fed her special shakes and special mac and cheese that was about three times the normal calorie count to compensate for her size. Years later, we realized she would develop just fine, and all that worry was wasted.

We are blessed in modern parenting to have milestones that we can measure, celebrate, and keep an eye on as our kids are growing up. In fact, failure to meet typical milestones is often what leads a parent to seek a diagnosis and early intervention. But as helpful as they are, too much emphasis on them can have you seeing the glass as half empty and feeling like your child is lacking.

While you want to be mindful of milestones, you also have to keep the big picture and the long term in mind. The worries many parents have about their child not walking, potty training, or even sleeping in their own bed by a certain age are usually forgotten by the time that child is a fully functional teenager, and none of that seems to matter. For any parent, it can be unhealthy to constantly compare your child to what others are doing. But for a parent raising a child with special needs, this can be super stressful and cause you to be less present to what is happening today.

Your child will be on a different path. It's okay to have goals and want to help them develop. But you must also live in the moment and make sure each day moves them a step closer to the goal to maximize their independence. One parent I spoke with shared a concept of "inch stones." The idea is that a child with special needs is going to progress slowly, and their changes will be more subtle. But if you are paying attention, those "inch stones" can be reasons to celebrate, high five, and dance around your house as if your child had just made the Olympics. Being able to celebrate every bit of progress was a universal key I heard when talking with parents.

GIVE YOUR CHILD THE GIFT OF EXPECTATIONS

When I spoke to adults who grew up with a disability, one of the main things they were thankful for is that their parents had expectations of them. It's important to not let your child with a disability get out of things like household chores, cleaning their room, or other things you'd expect of all your kids. You will likely have to adapt and give them tasks tailored to their abilities. But the idea is to have them grow up feeling like they, too, need to carry their weight around the house.

Several parents reported that kids with disabilities know how to "work" their parents to get out of doing work, just like any other kid. This can be especially true when the child is around others like grandparents. Be sure not to allow them to use their disability as a "get out of work" card. Kids are smart, and there is little more typical than trying to outsmart those around you and avoid hard work. If they struggle to do a task, give them an adapted version. They may be allowed to do a task differently or in a longer amount of time. But hold them accountable to doing the task. Don't let them get out of the work.

LET THEM LEARN BY BEING CHALLENGED

As a parent, it's tough to watch your child struggle. But one of the best things you can do is give them a safe space to stretch and be challenged. Kids learn from the consequences of their actions. The same is true for a child with a disability. For example, your child may struggle to put on their socks. It might take them fifteen minutes instead of just a few seconds. It will be hard to watch them struggle, and you must resist the temptation to swoop in and do it for them.

> But if you can step back and let them do it on their own, that is how they will learn.

One therapist gave a practical tip on working through challenges. They recommended picking and choosing the times to let your kid struggle. If your child is challenged by daily life skills like getting dressed, you might have to choose between getting them up super early to allow for extra time or letting them get enough sleep. It might make more sense to help them more in the morning so you can get out the door, and then set aside time at night to practice getting dressed with less time pressure. You also can match working on challenges with the mood and energy level of your child. Too much challenge at the wrong time can create undue pressure and lead to everyone having a bad moment.

Every adult I spoke with who grew up with a disability stressed when it comes to expectations, it is important to let your child fail. While it may seem cliche to say we learn more from our failures than our victories, it is definitely true when it comes to children and their development. "My mom let me try stuff, and a lot of times it didn't work out. I even had times where I fell flat on my face," explained Jimmy Kennedy, who has cerebral palsy. "But the best thing she gave me is that she let me fail. She let me learn from my mistakes and learn how to keep on pushing."

> Most parents said they struggled with the right balance of when to step in, and when to let their kids learn from the struggle.

"You have to be able to take little leaps of faith," explained Sue Schiavone, whose daughter Brittany has Down syndrome. "Brittany wanted to be able to get off the bus and let herself in our house after school with her own key like the other kids. I let her do it. I was around the corner watching, but I still let her do it." Create a safe space where your kids can stretch and even face setbacks with supports nearby if needed.

One parent shared what she called the "three-strike method" she had adapted from a book focused on kids who are very picky eaters. So often people see a child with a disability, and their automatic assumption is that they won't be able to do something. This is very unfair and opposite of the way we treat most kids. But with this three-strike method, the underlying assumption is to allow kids to assume they *can* do something—and it surely will not hurt to let them try. "First, you let them try. If they can't do it, that is strike one. Then you give them encouragement and allow them to try again. If they don't get the task, that is strike two. After the second try, then you offer an adapted way to do the same task." The mother reported that once she applied this method to just about everything in life, it took away the pressure and the worry about what her child could and could not do.

DON'T SET OR ACCEPT LIMITS

When Sophia's brother Peter was in lower school, he and his friends would wear NBA jerseys to school every day. They would play basketball at recess and pick the teams based on NBA jerseys. Peter is a University of Kentucky fan and was sure he would play one year for the Wildcats and then go pro as a "one and done" player. We faced a choice of squelching his dreams of the NBA and telling him it would never happen or letting him have a love of basketball that would bring him great experiences and shape part of his childhood. We chose to let him dream. He became a very good middle and high school player—but an even better runner.

He now runs at the college level, plays pickup basketball, and shoots video for all sports at his university. Those formative years as a fan, player, and teammate helped shape Peter into the young adult he is today. All kids have dreams, and all parents face that balancing act of letting their kids dream or steering them to shoot for something more practical. For parents of kids with special needs, this balance is key because a lot of the world is going to tell you all the things your child won't be able to do.

Never was this truer than with a young man I met in my days at the Kids Center named Willie Burton. Willie loved wrestling, and his dream was to become a wrestler. But Willie was a wheelchair user whose cerebral palsy impacted most of his body. That did not stop Willie from working his way onto his high school wrestling team. He worked out every day and had a determination that motivated his teammates. Every move they could make with ease was harder for Willie. But with determination and grit, he pushed on. He became an inspiration to his coach and teammates. They thought, if Willie is here pushing himself every day, then what excuse do I have to not work just as hard?

Willie would lose just about every match in high school. But despite going down to defeat time and time again, Willie would keep working, keep pushing, and keep showing up to battle. Finally, during his senior year in high school, he won one match. He ended with a high school record of just one win. His story is chronicled in a memoir about his life and was the focus of an ESPN E60 documentary. It was narrated by Dan Gable, a famous wrestler, whose college record in wrestling was the opposite of Willie's—just one loss. As Dan attested in the film, no matter how different their records were, they were both wrestlers.

> Your child's story may not be as dramatic as Willie's. But a lot of the world is going to try to define what will be possible for your child.

You may be told they will never be able to go to college, have a job, live independently, or get married. Most parents I talked with said they had a list they called the "never-ever" list of things they were told their child would not be able to do. And most found that many, if not all, of those things eventually got crossed off the list as their child developed.

One philosophy that rang true with many parents I interviewed was their kids weren't allowed to embrace "I can't" in their house while growing up. I also spoke with many adults who grew up with a disability who credited their parents with a spirit of adaptation instead of surrender. "*Can't* was not a word we accepted in our household. I would usually have to figure out a different way to do something, but I wasn't allowed to just give up and say I couldn't do it."

This was a universal theme when talking with young adults. An adult woman with a disability and limited use of her hands tells how she puts on a fancy dress and gets it zipped by herself in a real-world story of persistence and adaptation. This philosophy that *can't* is not in their vocabulary was a sort of internal rallying cry for just about every adult I spoke with who lives with a disability.

If you can let go of limiting thinking, you can allow your child to be happy where they are and still strive every day to have the best life possible. Dreams are not just for typically abled kids. Do not forget, your child's disability does not define who they are. It is a part of them that presents extra obstacles. Their future path will also be determined by other traits you passed down to them, as well as their own will and determination. If you are stubborn, chances are they might be too. Be careful what you wish for here, as teenagers with disabilities can be just as defiant as any other teen!

There are countless stories of the determination of the human spirit that helped people achieve things nobody ever thought were possible. Believe your child has that spirit within them, and allow them to aim high. Let them dream, and keep the focus on today being a great day that can help them take a step toward their dream. Regardless of where they end up, they will undoubtedly get further in life if they are allowed to focus on what they can do instead of thinking their world and their potential is limited by their disability.

DISCOVER YOUR CHILD'S ABILITIES

When you are raising a child with special needs, no matter how positive you are, life is going to be focused on helping them overcome their deficits. Even though it's not your intention, life is going to be about helping them work on the things they can't do. Therapy can feel this way. You will no doubt work with amazing therapists who have great knowledge, great passion for their work, and an ability to push your child—and you—past their comfort zone. But therapy can tend to focus on overcoming deficits. That's why it is important to discover early what your child does enjoy, as well as the natural skills they have.

Expose your kids to lots of different activities, and pay attention to what seems to bring them joy. This is a process for all parents to discover whether their child is drawn more to reading, music, the debate team, outdoor activities and sports, or anything else. Luckily, today there are countless activities and programs that are either for mixed ability levels or are separate and totally adaptive. Not only will you and your child discover what motivates them, but these activities will help them take things like therapy and apply them to the real world. It will also boost their self-esteem and increase their social connections. As a parent, being involved in activities will connect you to another layer of your village.

CELEBRATE EVERY STEP ON THE NEW JOURNEY

When you let go of what you thought life was going to be, you can now imagine a new path and a new future for your child. If you can resist the temptation to worry or set limits, you can create a path for your child with new and different expectations.

Having a child with a disability can make getting through an average day a lot of work. But one good side effect of this is being more present with the little things that happen each day. And this also means celebrating every gain along the way.

You can be a big guide to help your child reach their potential. Try not to be too overprotective. Give them room to experience life like any other child. Don't let comparison rob you of celebrating your child's progress. Help your child be stronger by giving them expectations and letting them fail. Don't set a cap on what is possible for them. Remove *can't* from their vocabulary, and teach them to find a way around obstacles. This can-do spirit will help them be as independent as possible as young adults.

ABILITY EVERYONE CAN SEE

Inam Shalati and her parents were told again and again what she'd never be able to do. When she was born three months early, they were told she might not live. She was born blind but also had limited mobility due to cerebral palsy that impacted all four of her limbs. The odds were stacked against Inam from the start.

What she did have was a sharp mind and fearless determination. She learned braille at age six and excelled in school. Early on it was clear Inam had a giving spirit and a passion to help others with disabilities. She started volunteering at age fourteen by mentoring other blind young people. She became a speaker, going into schools and helping kids learn about blindness and cerebral palsy.

> "I wanted to let the kids know that people are people first, not just people with a disability. I wanted them to know that people with disabilities have a lot to offer the world."

As an adult, Inam continued her passion for helping others. For over nine years she was a volunteer making phone calls to seniors to check in on them each day. "I would make my calls, and then the organization would give me the overflow for other volunteers who could not handle their assignments." She volunteered for the Recording House for the Blind. When I worked at the Kids Center, she volunteered for us, raising money with a team in our Walk and making calls for events.

In 1999, Inam was honored with the Bell Award, a prestigious volunteer award given at a fancy gala put on by a local TV station in Louisville, Kentucky. The list of fellow Bell Award winners reads like the Who's Who of Philanthropy in the community. In 2009, she met children's music singer Dave Kinoin. Dave was so taken by Inam's spirit that he wrote several songs about her, including "She Won't Stop Giving" and more. Inam's story has also been featured in numerous publications, such as the *Braille Monitor* and more.

In recent years, Inam battled cancer and several other health issues. But she never let obstacles stop her from helping others. Today, she helps local restaurants by translating their menus into braille, and she still makes the calls to seniors. When it was time to have her as a guest on my *Seeing Ability* podcast, she refused to reschedule and recorded her episode from her hospital bed. Inam has boundless energy and always has a smile in her voice and on her face. Although she may be blind, she sees the ability in every person more than most.

Many parents are told what their kids won't be able to do. If you are reading this book, you or someone you know has or likely will experience this. Kids hear it too. Inam Shalati and her parents heard it all the time. But she was deaf to the noise and determined to push past obstacles. She chose to use what she could do instead of focusing on her limitations. And she has put her talents to work for the good of others.

8 ADVOCATING FOR YOUR CHILD'S EDUCATION

When you get through the initial stages of adjusting to this path, you start building a future for your child. Before long, that future involves helping your child get a good education.

We had no idea if Sophia would have lasting cognitive impacts from her premature birth. We didn't know if she'd learn differently or need special assistance. Early on, we explored private schools, thinking smaller class sizes would allow individualized attention.

I will never forget when we visited one very well-respected school in Louisville. Once we told them that Sophia had cerebral palsy, they immediately said we might want to hold her back since she might have trouble keeping up at grade level with kids her age. This was shocking to us, because having CP does not automatically mean the child will have cognitive delays. Like most diagnoses, every child is different. In Sophia's case, despite fluid buildup on her brain in the NICU, she's always been quite smart and gets mostly A's. The fact that this highly educated head of school just assumed her CP meant learning delays was an eye-opener.

For the most part, Sophia's K-12 school journey was that of a typically abled child. In high school, we realized she took a bit longer to process and had her qualify for time accommodations on testing. This took her test grades up a notch. We also had her retake the ACT with accommodations. If you know Sophie, you will realize that no amount of time is going to turn her into a math whiz. But with extra time on the English section, she scored a perfect score of thirty-six. I like to say I married up, and Sophia takes after my wife! Just like medicine, the journey for education is one of learning, finding your voice, advocacy, and training your child to push for all they are due in education.

BECOME KNOWN AT SCHOOL

In order for your child to get what they need, you are going to have to advocate for them at each stage. This might make you run the risk of being "that parent" who is seen as pushy, demanding, and never satisfied.

That is why it's vital for the school to know you as more than just the parent of a special needs child. Get involved at school. Volunteer and offer to help whenever possible. There is something magical that happens when you are working side by side with someone to set up tables, staff a booth, put away chairs, sweep the floor, and get everything put back just the way it was. You get to talk to parents and teachers about everything else in the world besides disabilities. Let them get to know you and your entire family. Allow the teachers and administrators to see your softer, more vulnerable side. Find out about them, their interests, their families, and their hobbies outside of school.

TALK TO OTHERS IN THE SAME BOAT

Just like navigating the world of medicine, in regards to education, most parents don't even know what they don't know. I recommend turning to organizations that helped you create your village. They can connect you to other parents whose children have the same diagnosis so you can pick their brains about schooling. Find parents with children who are the same age and some who are a few years older who have been through what you are facing now. Ask them what they learned the hard way, what they'd do over if they could, and so on. Most nonprofits will have advice and resources when it comes to education. Some may even have workshops, webinars, and classes. Find a teacher in your network—family, friends, and others—who can help you decipher the lingo and who knows a bit more about how the system works.

GET YOUR CHILD TO BE AS INCLUDED AS POSSIBLE WITH OTHERS

The goal should always be to have your child as main-streamed as possible, where they are in a regular classroom. Every child is different. Some may thrive better in a more separated environment. Remember, the end goal is to help your child become an independent adult. This is why having them as integrated as possible during their education is key.

> You are going to have to advocate for inclusion, because others may not.

In some cases, teachers may be protective of students and worry they won't have the support they need in a regular class setting. It also is harder to schedule and staff for your child to be in a different setting or to even move between settings. Finally, when you ask your child to stretch outside their comfort zone, it might trigger them to act out, thus making them harder to support. This is why the easiest path of keeping them separate may be the choice offered, if you are not the one advocating for more.

You might get the recommendation for your child to leave a segmented classroom for specialty learning areas, such as art, music, or PE. Think through whether it's the right fit for your child. Consider the teacher in that specialty area. Ask if the teacher in that area is rigid or flexible. Ask if they are good at helping kids work through behavioral issues.

Be sure to consider the learning environment. For example, one mom I spoke with said her child was sent out for PE. This ended up being the worst setting, because without structure and physical boundaries, her son was a "runner" and had to be chased down by the teacher. For him, it might have been better to be sent out to a math class. Even if he was performing at a different level, the structure and the contained space of a physical classroom would help him have a higher chance of thriving. You know your child best. You know what they can tolerate and what type of environment will interfere with their ability to learn.

Keep in mind that the best environment for your child may change with age and phase of school. One mom said she spent years fighting for inclusion in lower levels, but then decided to switch to a specialized school in middle school. Suddenly she found she was less stressed, was not always fighting the system, and her child had more time to devote to outside things such as choir, soccer, and other activities. There is no one answer. Seek input from your therapists, teachers, doctors, and your child.

LEARN HOW TO GET THE MOST OUT OF YOUR CHILD'S EDUCATION PLAN

There are few things more important regarding the educational journey than what schools call an "individualized education plan"—or IEP. I spoke at length with parents, teachers, and administrators to get advice on best practices that help teachers and parents support your child.

> The first piece of advice was to avoid an "us versus them" mindset and to see the IEP as a collaboration and a team effort.

When you approach the meeting as if it's a battle, you tend to have everyone in the room react in a more defensive and possibly even confrontational way. If you let educators know that you appreciate them, are willing to work with them, and your goal is to work as a team to help the child, then you will set a positive framework.

Keep in mind how long you will have a relationship with your child's school. "If you go in there and every meeting seems like a fight, and your child is six or seven years old, you have a long road in front of you," explained one mother. "They are not going anywhere, and you are going to be working with them for many years. You have to find a way to advocate for your child and push for what you know they need, but do so in a way that does not seem like a confrontation."

DO YOUR HOMEWORK BEFORE YOU GO

Your meetings with the school will be more successful if you do some homework and walk in prepared. The school team will also treat you differently if it's clear you know what you are talking about. It also helps when they see you have a full understanding of the process. Tell them your number-one goal is the success of your child. But also let them know you see things from a team point of view, not just from the parent's side.

Start by making sure you are organized. Most parents used binders to keep track of old IEP documents, evaluations, and correspondence. Lean on the skills and strengths of your partner or those who are part of your extended team. If you are bad at paperwork, find a friend or family member who can be your organizational ace. Ask for a blank copy of the IEP template so you can know what to expect ahead of time.

Like many points on this parenting journey, the IEP is a great chance to reach out to your village and find other parents who have gone before you. Ask them for tips, lessons learned, things they would do differently if they had the chance. Some parents I spoke with said they reduced anxiety about the meeting by asking an advocate or a friend familiar with the process to do a "mock" IEP with them. There are also many resources online on the topic, including articles, videos, and more.

The school will send a written notice of the meeting that includes who will be in attendance. You will want to make sure the right people are in the room. You want the people who can move the needle in a given area to be in the room with you. Consider taking another person with you to the meeting, such as an advocate, a therapist, or even a teacher who knows your child. Be sure those people do not take over the meeting but are there to support you. They should embody a spirit of collaboration and cooperation instead of conflict. You want them to be a sort of interpreter, a resource but not akin to having an attorney in the room to battle the "opposite side." Maintain the tone that everyone is part of one big team with your child's needs as the bond that ties you together.

Get clear on what you want to ask for and what your child needs.

Send a written notice of your requests ahead of time, so the school knows what you are asking for. Instead of presenting a list of what you want, or worse yet what you are demanding, make a case for why you feel your child needs various items on the list so they can thrive in the school and realize their potential. This keeps the focus on what is best for the child, not what you are asking for.

If you have evaluations or other input, be sure to send it before the meeting. Ask for a draft of the IEP so you can review it before the meeting. Think about it—the teachers have put in time to draft and coordinate a thoughtful plan. It puts you at a disadvantage if you are seeing that plan for the first time in the meeting and reacting to it on the spot.

To help meet your child's needs, you will want to come prepared with your own ideas and solutions instead of just asking the school to figure it out. This is where some good old-fashioned research about what works in schools would help you educate yourself on the subject. Talk to other parents, teachers, and therapists, and get their ideas to meet your child's needs and challenges. So many parents I talked with shared how other parents gave them simple ideas—call them "hacks"—that often were well received and even incorporated by the school. For example, one parent I spoke with knew her son was very smart but was stuck on how he could take a spelling test since he was mostly nonverbal and struggled to hold a pencil. The team brainstormed ideas and tried writing several versions of the word, having him pick the correct one. Then a member of the team gave him letters so he could arrange them and spell the word. This allowed him to show his knowledge even though he did not speak and had trouble writing.

Take an honest, objective look at your child, and don't set limits. But by the same token, if you come into the meetings with the belief your child is good at everything and has no areas where they struggle, you will seem unreasonable. Let the school team know you are aware of your child's weaknesses, their deficits, and where they are challenged. This shows you are not just a biased parent, but you can step back and look objectively at the situation.

But by the same token, nobody knows the strengths of your child quite like you. There might be things they are capable of that they only do at home because the school environment causes them to shut down. Make a summary of your child's strengths *and* weaknesses. Include an explanation of their learning styles and things you know they need to succeed. Just as importantly, it can be helpful to let the team know of triggers or environments when your child is not at their best. Brainstorm possible solutions to your child's needs, and get it all on paper. One mom I spoke with updates an "about me" page for her daughter each year. This way any teacher, substitute, or aide can read a one-page summary of her child. She shared that school staff love the tool and wish they had it for all students.

TIPS DURING YOUR IEP MEETING

Now that you've done your preparation, it's time to sit down for the meeting. Remember, an IEP is going to focus on the gap between where your child is today and where you and the school team want them to be. Everyone in the room is a fan of your kid, is rooting for them, and could make a list of positive things to say about your child.

However, IEP meetings focus on deficits. Realize this. If you don't, it's very easy for these meetings to feel very negative, because as the parent, all you are hearing is what your child can't do. Most people I talked with relayed how hard it was to constantly hear what your child is not doing and to not take it personally, to not get defensive, depressed, or angry. Starting with the right framework for the meeting and the right mindset to approach it in a positive way is probably the best advice I received.

There are certain keys to success with such meetings. They go well when all parties have done a great deal of preparation. Successful IEPs had a spirit of teamwork instead of an "us versus them" mindset. It also helped when everyone in the room appreciated the fact that schools have limits on what they can provide, even if they wanted to do more. Finally, meetings go better when there is a broader and healthy relationship with the school outside of just the IEP setting. Meetings break down when parents come in angry, overly demanding, and when the focus of the meeting is about who to blame instead of how to figure out what is best for the child.

If you find yourself hitting a roadblock during the meeting, one IEP advocate I spoke to suggested asking the following questions:

- Why are you recommending this?
- Why can't we do what I am requesting?
- Is there another possible solution we might all consider?

When the meeting wraps up, ask the team to read the summary notes aloud to ensure they captured the conversation the way you remember it. Most parents recommended not formally signing off on the IEP until you had been given a written copy and have had the time to fully review it.

The road to help your child with a disability navigate the world of learning and education is not a simple one. There isn't one way to get there or one path to take. The path you do take will not be a straight line. There will be detours, pit stops, and maybe even a breakdown along the way. The key will depend on your level of knowledge, your attitude and philosophy, and the degree to which you can find an atmosphere where you feel like a team that collaborates and works well together for the good of your child.

CHANGING PERSPECTIVES

From the moment Jackie Diaz babysat her cousin with Down syndrome, she knew she wanted to become a special-education teacher. For twelve years, she worked in the classroom and got to know the needs of students and parents. Then she made a switch to school administration and today is a principal who leads all educators, including those who do special ed.

With years of experience and training, she thought she had a good understanding of the challenges parents faced and the ways to help parents and their kids succeed.

That got turned on its head when her son Owen was born. Early on, he had hearing challenges. When doing a hearing evaluation, she was not prepared to learn Owen had autism that impeded his learning. "It changes when it's your kid. My mind started to race, and I was wondering what his future would be like. Would he always live with me?" Like most parents, Jackie was flooded with emotion. She tried to look at her son in a new way to discover who he was and what he needed. But doing so made her feel distant from her own child she so adored. That feeling of distance made her feel alone, scared, and even ashamed.

Jackie paused and, instead of worrying about his entire life, started to focus on what was next to help Owen. "Having a diagnosis didn't change me or change Owen. But it changed what was next. It for sure wasn't the same as when I raised my first child," she explained. "I was used to being in control. And for the first time in my life, I didn't know where to go. So I started to do a lot of education." From then on, life became about figuring out the next part of the journey.

When she had her first meeting about Owen with the school team, Jackie knew what to expect. After all, at that point she had sat through literally thousands of these meetings and had been the facilitator of many herself. Sitting in the same room on the other side of the table opened her eyes to what she didn't know. "I know the meetings go through what a kid can and cannot do. But I had no idea how it felt to sit there and hear about all his deficits. Of course, I already knew those things. Nobody knows Owen better than me. But I have to admit it was soul-crushing to be bombarded with item after item. I just had no idea what it felt like to hear that about your child."

Jackie's advice to educators is to slow down and make sure the parents understand everything you are discussing and what you are recommending. She also wants educators to try to offer their best and treat each child as if they were their own.

For parents, Jackie advises you go into school meetings seeking solutions and not looking for a fight. She also recommends that you never stop learning and that you never accept the answer of "This is all we have." "Keep searching. Keep pushing. Because if you don't push, who else is going to?" If a school can't give you what you desire, Jackie recommends asking what they *can* do that gets as close to your true desire as possible.

Acceptance of this new path is not a one-time event, and be prepared that it may hit you again and again at various stages of your child's life. Finally, Jackie reminds parents to never be so caught up in the struggle that they forget to stop and experience the moments of pure joy.

9 THE ROAD LESS TRAVELED

I really didn't know what to expect when Sophia was on the way. I didn't expect to fear losing my wife and my daughter. I can remember that sense of panic like it was yesterday. They both made it, and we found ourselves on a new and unexpected path. Those ten weeks in the NICU were terrifying. The birth of your child is supposed to be a celebration. Ours was a tense and exhausting two-and-a-half-month blur. We had so much help, starting with the nurses and doctors who took care of Sophia when we could not be there.

In those first years, we had a parade of therapists bring services to our doorstep. We went on the road with back-and-forth trips multiple times a week to the Kids Center for therapy, which became our new home away from home.

I met many amazing people in those early years. We will never forget Miss Bonny and Miss Amy, our physical therapist and occupational therapist. They didn't just treat Sophia; they loved her. They held our hands as parents to let us know everything was going to be okay. We met other parents who reassured us and shared the tips they had picked up along the way. We attended social events and fundraisers together. Here, our kids were normal, and we felt at ease. Being around other families also reminded us how lucky we were and just how much worse Sophia could have been.

TODAY SOPHIA IS A CAPABLE, BEAUTIFUL, AND INDEPENDENT YOUNG WOMAN.

She went to college at Loyola Chicago and fell in love with the Windy City. She stayed there and has an apartment on the north side of Chicago. She loves to read, go to concerts, cook, and play with Earl, her adorable cat. She works as a barista in a fancy, independent coffee shop. She has short hair, a few piercings, and a few more tattoos than Mom or Dad would prefer. I do not think she will ever leave the energy and diversity of the big city. This gives us a great excuse to take many trips a year to Chicago, which LeAnn and I love.

> Today, even though she had such a rough start and will always have CP, the day-to-day impact on her life is minimal.

Her vision issues as a preemie have always left her with thick glasses and very poor eyesight. She does not drive, which thankfully is okay if you live in a big city with a lot of public transportation. While she will always have less flexibility and more tightness on her left side, she walks a lot every day and is able to do so without issue.

She does struggle with anxiety, which could be related to her "wiring" being different as a result of being born so prematurely. We are all aware Sophia dodged a bullet and could have had many more lasting impacts from her early birth. In our house, it's not hyperbole to call her our "miracle baby."

LEANN AND I LEARNED A LOT ABOUT PARENTING AND LIFE ALONG THE WAY.

I am an even-keeled person who tends to roll with the punches. I now know I need to thank my parents for instilling in me a sense of calm and confidence that, no matter the storm, I would be able to see my way through. That calm confidence helped me in those early years. LeAnn and I also learned to lean on each other and to allow vulnerability. We learned to be more present and soak in every moment. We learned to have patience and to give everyone grace, including ourselves.

> We had to realize not everything comes according to plan, but in the end, it usually does come.

Life is indeed a journey with no guarantees. Sophia's emergency birth and related issues put us on a different path. But we have discovered it's less about which path you are on and more about the journey.

I hope sharing our story and the lessons I learned from others will help you and those you know greatly. The road you are on is likely not at all what you expected. But if you are open to what it can bring you, I believe it will be one of discovery, love, and pure joy. It won't be easy. It won't be without struggle, setback, and even heartache. But I have yet to meet anyone whose path was. In the end, it's about your mindset and those you choose to have in your village. I truly feel with the right mindset and the right people, any path can be one of love and joy.

And now that we have met, I consider each of you part of my village forever.

10 DON'T STOP BELIEVIN'

So much of the path raising a child who is different is filled with a focus on what they can't or might not be able to do. It's easy to be afraid and worried. However, when you talk to families on this path, you realize the joy felt by every single parent who has traveled it. You see how kids are beating the odds every single day. I could likely fill a hundred pages with stories of kids whose parents were told they would not live, would not walk, would not talk, and so on. They celebrate each time their child does another thing many thought impossible.

Below are a few of those stories to bring you a smile and fill your heart with hope for your child. To read other stories, visit seeingability.com, or listen to the Seeing Ability Podcast.

Mary Perkins was not supposed to live past childhood. Mary and her parents, John and Kim, live in Oxford, Ohio. She had multiple brain surgeries as a young child to remove cancerous tumors. She was given very little chance of survival; the surgeries left her with limited use of her left arm and leg and blind in one eye. Mary is now twenty years old and a college sophomore. She has been on dozens of hikes with Luke5 Adventures, even to epic places like Rocky

Mountain National Park and Israel. She has been to 10,000 feet above sea level and 1,400 feet below sea level. She says, "I hiked to the top of that mountain." She does not say, "My friends carried me to the top."

Linda Manning was told by her parents she would always need assistance due to her cerebral palsy. Today she celebrates "little miracles" of being able to dress herself and take care of herself. She also got married, something her family never dreamed was possible.

When Cameron and Jessica found out their son **Brooks Howell** had SMARD (Spinal Muscular Atrophy with Respiratory Distress) the research said he'd likely die before the age of two. Today at age five, Brooks is *very* happy and healthy, goes to school with his nurse three days a week, and loves his family, friends, and teachers! He is afraid of nothing. His parents are inspired and see him as a blessing and a gift. The fact that Brooks faces countless medical procedures with a smile has his parents in awe. They never thought they would get to see how much fun he has socializing with his friends and teachers at school and church. Brooks loves people. This allows his parents to feel like there's hope for him to have a somewhat "normal" social life as he gets older. It also warms their heart to see so many "typical" kids with a genuine interest in those with disabilities.

Kaylee Quinn Sipe has faced many medical challenges in her thirteen years, having been born with hemimegaloencephaly and epilepsy (infantile spasms, tonic clonic and complex partial seizures), left hemiparesis, anhidrosis, cognitive delay, apraxia of speech, expressive speech delays, fine/gross motor delays. She also has juvenile osteochondritis dissecans in both knees. Her mother, Geri, is amazed that she has been able thus far to be surgery free and regulated by medicine. Her mom loves to watch her achieve in life, like coloring or reading a page out loud at her level of reading ability. She's a doer of great things without needing to be recognized. Kaylee also loves helping others and her family. When she first asked to try to swallow her medications, that took her to an even greater level of independence. She challenged herself to try one, then another. All meds are pill based now!

Three-year-old **Brielle** suffered from a nonaccidental traumatic brain injury, cerebral palsy, and seizures. At five months old, her mother was told she may never walk or talk, may be blind, and would likely not be able to attach to her mom because she had never had a healthy attachment. She was a near fatality, and they were still unsure if she would need further brain surgeries. When she was eight months old, Brielle was discharged from neurology, even though previously, doctors thought she'd have to have surgery. At eighteen months old, she took her first steps, and she has not stopped there. Today, this miracle girl runs in her yard with her brother, advocates for herself with her voice, and gives the very best hugs and kisses. She loves to cuddle before bed each night with her mother and bubba (brother).

Luke Feger is the youngest of Stephanie and Cory's three kids and was diagnosed with sensory processing disorder when he was in preschool. Luke was never told he wasn't capable, but pre-COVID, his school had made the frustrating decision to not let him move forward because of his inability to sit in a circle on the floor. They made multiple excuses to hold him back and began to stereotype him instead of love him for who he was. But Luke didn't let others hold him back, even if they wanted to. COVID hit, and Stephanie chose to homeschool their whole family exclusively for two years. During that time, Luke was doing classwork with his sister, twenty months older than him. During that time, Stephanie learned a lot about how Luke learned, how his character shows up, and how she could best show up for him. Now, years later, he's academically nailing it, socially on par, and while the family still navigates some of the sensory-seeking behaviors, together they are learning how to tackle any hurdle he faces with grace, courage, and determination.

Hunter Baynum was born in northern Kentucky and diagnosed at age two with autism, and at the time, he was nonverbal. Today, Anna, Hunter's mom, shares her child is one the teacher praises every year for making friends with anyone and standing up for others, both in and out of the classroom! She will never forget the day she first heard him sing a song along with the radio. Music has always been a huge part of her own life and was always on in their home. One day, he started to sing along to "I Just Can't Wait to Be King" from *The Lion King*. They listened to it every day for a month just so she could hear him sing and talk.

John Cronin's family never set limits on John because of his Down syndrome. They started a company called "John's Crazy Socks," today the largest sock store in the US! John and his father, Mark, travel around the country inspiring others to not set limits on children just because they are different. John has served on the board of the National Down Syndrome Society and their company has donated over $700,000 to charities by giving five percent of their sales each year.

Society will tell you kids with Down syndrome won't be productive citizens. They are very wrong. **Elijah Shown**, now nineteen years old, volunteers with us regularly and does good throughout the city. Going to IEP meetings were always hard, and they made his parents feel like they were not doing enough because they heard how he's only able to do this or that and not at a certain level. Elijah had a hard time writing and didn't like it, but today he is able to write, and you're able to read it—something that makes him feel he's like everyone else. In middle school, Elijah told his parents he wanted to go to college. At the time, they thought he already wanted what others want, but they weren't sure how this was going to happen. Today, through the local school system, he is attending his favorite college, the University of Louisville, and is absolutely loving it. He feels more like a grown-up and is becoming more and more independent every day. His parents feel so proud of him, but more than that, he is proud to be there. Go Cards!

Jacob Chad Meshell was born to Brad and Jaime Meshell in Nashville, Tennessee. Because of his autism diagnosis at five years old, Jacob's parents were told speech would be his biggest challenge, that Jacob would struggle to communicate his thoughts and emotions. They were also told Jacob could be dependent on them for the rest of his life. But when Jacob says, "I love you, Daddy," and then kisses him goodnight, it is magical. Brad never thought he would experience those words or emotions. It makes him cry to even consider it. Brad believes Jacob knows how much he is loved. Brad and Jaime have hugged and kissed him since birth, and they believe he knows what love is. He will now just approach and hug them and jump in their lap. He will grab their hands and lead them around just to walk with them. Brad feels like he will break through at any moment and take control of his world! Keep winning, Jacob!

Kylie Smallwood is fifteen years old now and lives with cerebral palsy that impacts the right side of her body due to a stroke she suffered as a child. Her diagnosis makes it hard to walk or run, ride a bike, tie her own shoes, or do anything two-handed. But Kylie walked at nine months old and started riding a bike with no training wheels at six years old. By second grade, she was determined and used *both* hands to tie her own shoes. She was a cheerleader for three years, ran cross-country for three years, and played volleyball. She loves to bake and cook, she *can* do everyday tasks, and she adapts or adjusts to do what she needs to. Kylie is excelling at her high school Cambridge classes, and she is also taking classes to pursue a career in nursing. Every milestone is huge because Kylie conquers, perseveres, and lets nothing stop her. She believes in herself, and if she wants something, she'll make it happen.

Early on, Karen and David decided their son, **Caleb Prewitt**, would not be limited by society, by doctors, by educators, by anyone due to his Down syndrome diagnosis. They included him in as many community activities and events as fit on their calendars and, in the process, met many interesting and supportive people along the way. As a result, Caleb became used to being in different settings, trying new experiences, and having an irregular schedule. His involvement in sports brought that all to a new level, though. In 2020, he learned to ride a bike and took up running and swimming. In 2021, he completed his first triathlon, becoming the youngest person with Down syndrome to do so. Since then, he has traveled the country participating in multi-sport events, meeting new friends, and he is truly living his best life. He's completed 35 triathlons to date, with many more on the calendar. He's begun to deliver presentations, has represented the Down syndrome community at events, and has even joined Team USA to head to Spain in 2025. Karen and David are proud of his determination and effort, but most importantly, Caleb is proud of himself and his accomplishments!

When God called Sonia to work in at a nonprofit that provided services and support for individuals with disabilities, she didn't imagine that 17 years later she'd have a granddaughter with physical and mental challenges. **Haley** was diagnosed with autism at the age of two. Sonia can't count the number of nights she travelled to her daughter's house and sat in tears as Haley banged her head uncontrollably on the walls and floors. Haley had so much she wanted to express and tell but was nonverbal. During one speech therapy session, Haley was so frustrated two minutes in that she began to bang her head, leaving all in tears. Sonia remembers the words the therapist said: "Don't you worry. If she only gives me two minutes each session, I will take it. We will build on it. And you see this speech device we are working on; one day you will donate it back." Because Sonia worked in this field for many years, she had faith in the therapist's words. Haley did find her own voice at the age of five with the help of many therapists and teachers. Sonia calls them all Haley's special angels.

When your child continues to prove the naysayers incorrect, it's always something to be celebrated. May these testimonies bring you hope that your child will conquer their own list of "never-evers."

Enjoy stories of other families on this path by visiting seeingability.com and listening to the Seeing Ability Podcast.

ACKNOWLEDGMENTS

This book could never have been written without the input from those I interviewed. I can never thank you enough—the parents, the adults, the therapists, the doctors, the educators, and the nonprofit leaders—for pouring out your hearts, your souls, and sometimes even your tears to me. I took it as a sacred honor to convey your passion, your emotion, your joy, your heartbreak, and your wisdom so others might learn from it.

A special thanks to my editorial board, who looked at my manuscript and gave me valuable input. Thank you, Cameron Howell, Jamie Ramsay, Sarah Richardson, Sonia Johnson, Samantha Fields, and Dr. Ron Lehocky.

Speaking of writing, I could not have done this process without the guidance of Stephanie Feger and her team. As a special-needs mama, she gets this book. Thank you for taking ownership of something so important to me and helping coach me along the way.

While my mom is no longer with us, this book would not be complete without a tribute to her and my dad. They always loved reading my writing and encouraged me in whatever path I chose in life. It took many years for that path to return to writing, but their encouragement made me believe that even at an older age, I could produce something that would move people. There is little that can replace a parent having confidence in their child and that child believing that they can do *anything* they put their mind to because of their support.

I can't check off a bucket list item without thanking my long-time friend Stacey Vicari. Her worldview and her friendship have shaped the way I see the world for over thirty-five years. My life has never been the same since she came into it. The "best person" at my wedding, I will never be able to adequately thank her for her influence on my path.

Few people embody the spirit of "ability" like Inam Shalati. I don't know anyone else who called me almost every day wanting to know when the book would be done so she could make sure we created a braille version—which she got funded through her tenacity and never being afraid to ask for what she wants. Thanks for always giving to others, Miss Inam.

I am so lucky my best friend is still my girlfriend after twenty-seven years. I tell people I definitely "married up," and it is true in more ways than she will ever know. Thank you, my sweet LeAngela, for always believing in me. Thanks, too, for letting me let people into our story with this book.

I was blessed that my love for LeAnn created two beautiful children. So different, yet both so wonderful. I am most proud they are good people who others love to be around. Sophia and Peter, I could not be more proud to be your dad.

ABOUT THE AUTHOR

Jim Littlefield-Dalmares has been using storytelling to help others for over thirty years. As a marketing and fundraising professional, Jim helped change lives working for his local United Way, as well as a national environmental charity. For over a decade, he advocated for children with special needs as head of marketing and fundraising for the Kids Center for Pediatric Therapies in Louisville, Kentucky. He is an avid giver, serving on boards, counseling nonprofits, and mentoring through Big Brother/Big Sisters.

Today, he hosts a podcast called *Seeing Ability*. Each month, Jim shines the spotlight on individuals with special needs and their families. He includes a monthly charity spotlight episode that showcases those doing good work for people with special needs. Jim is the founder of the Seeing Ability Foundation, Inc., which offers a variety of support to families traveling the path of a special-needs parent.

ABOUT THE SEEING ABILITY PODCAST

True learning comes from hearing diverse perspectives.

The Seeing Ability Podcast is a dedicated space for people with disabilities and those who support them. Through honest conversations and inspiring stories, Jim Littlefield-Dalmares aims to create a valuable resource that educates, empowers, and builds a strong, supportive community that celebrates the unique abilities within us all. Whether you are an individual with a disability or a parent, therapist, medical professional, educator, nonprofit leader or another supporter, this podcast is for you.

Join us as we explore the challenges and triumphs of the disability community, share practical advice, and foster a network of understanding and encouragement. Each episode is designed to provide insights, inspire action, and highlight the incredible potential within every person. Subscribe to the Seeing Ability Podcast and be a part of a movement that sees beyond limitations and embraces the extraordinary.

Visit seeingability.com to learn more or listen to the podcast on your favorite podcast listening platform.

ABOUT THE FOUNDATION

Where some see challenge, we see opportunity. Where some see hardships, we see potential. Where some see ordinary, we see extraordinary. Where some see disabilities, we see unique abilities.

The Seeing Ability Foundation, Inc., is a 501(c)(3) nonprofit organization dedicated to transforming lives by celebrating and empowering every individual's potential. Its mission is to support families raising children with differing abilities by creating a strong, supportive community and offering essential resources, education, and empowerment for their journey.

The foundation funds impactful initiatives such as the Seeing Ability Podcast, which shares inspiring stories and expert insights from diverse voices within the disability community, and donates copies of *Seeing Ability* to schools, nonprofits, hospitals, clinics, and therapy centers—serving as a valuable resource and needed inspiration to families and professionals working with children with disabilities.

Become a part of making a difference—your support, whether personal or through your business, helps sustain our projects and launch new initiatives that uplift and empower families. For more information on how to get involved, visit seeingability.com.

APPENDIX 1

A BREATH FOR SOPHIA

This is taken from an email I sent three days after Sophia was born. It got spread around, and some lady I never met set up a web page for us and posted it. This was 2000, so you have to remember that use of the internet was new. This was before Facebook and other such sites that make sharing stories easier today. The post got replies from people around the globe. I will never be able to thank those people for what their love meant to us in that moment.

Here is the email.

―――

PLEASE READ

If you're like me, you get a lot of emails from friends who forward things to everybody. As an activist, I get several a day asking me to call, or write, or protest, or sign my name. I realize that on a busy day, you might be tempted to click "delete" and get rid of this email right away.

I ask you to take about 3-5 minutes of your very valuable time to use the internet as a tool for healing.

A BREATH FOR SOPHIA

My request is simple: Take a few moments today—maybe even right now—to breathe deeply, focus on a few key thoughts, and share a bit of your life force for a very special little girl.

Her name is Sophia (or Sophie), and she is our tiny daughter, born 1 lb. 9 oz last Saturday, March 4, 2000 (at 26 weeks) as my wife battled with a severe and surprise case of preeclampsia/toxemia. (My wife is recovering fine, by the way.)

As with most preemies, Sophia has a long road of many battles ahead of her. But her first and perhaps most critical battle is with underdeveloped and diseased lungs which, as of today, do not allow her to breathe without the aid of a ventilator.

Thus the importance of the breath, our very life force. Please take a moment and take a few deep breaths with me:

1. **Take a breath and be thankful for your own health.** Be glad you are alive enough to walk, to run, to dance, to play, to work, to help, to age, to love, to cry, and even to feel life's aches and pains.
2. **Take a breath and be thankful for your family.** Hug your children. Adore your spouse. Honor your elders. Reach out to relatives. Set aside your differences long enough to realize the love all around you.
3. **Take a breath for our planet and all life on it.** From the rivers to the ozone, from the lizards to us humans, celebrate the resilient and vibrant will of life to go on.
4. **Share a breath for the children.** Of course, Sophia is just one of millions of children who need our prayers and hopes. Breathe so they may get a fair start in life.
5. **Share a breath with Sophia.** As you breathe, send a thought/say a prayer/send good energy her way. Perhaps if we all give her a little, we can put some air behind her sails.

May you be granted peace, health, and happiness. Thanks for a few minutes today. If you desire, please share this email with others. Right now, we can use all the hopes and prayers out there.

Jim :-)

Jim Littlefield-Dalmares
A new father

APPENDIX 2

HOW OTHERS CAN HELP

The first thing that trips parents up is not having a list of needs, but actually being willing to ask for and be okay with receiving help. Too often, we try to be that super parent who can do it all. Below is a list of ideas I got from my own experience and the interviews I did with parents. As I get more ideas from podcast guests and people that I interview for my blog, I will be sure to add them to my website. Lists are great, but only if you commit to being okay with the idea of asking for help!

MEDICAL

Paperwork Tamer: Find that friend or family member whose office is full of well-organized file folders with neat labels. They can help you keep track of medical records as well as statements from insurance companies.

Appointment Buddy: You will be glad you took someone with you to every appointment who could take notes and be an unemotional observer.

Translator: Search your network for a doctor or a nurse who can help you decipher medical jargon. It's a game-changer when you speak their language.

Therapy Team: Sometimes the hardest thing to know is what you don't know. Ask therapists and teachers for a list of questions to ask at each medical appointment.

Sibling Sitter: You may have times when you need to go overnight with your child, which means you need someone to watch the other kids. This can be a friend or family member.

HOUSEHOLD

Cleaning: Swallow your pride and let your friend or family member come in every so often and clean your house. They may not be around to do this every month for years. So when they *are* willing, take them up on the offer.

Meals: At the start, you might have more trays of lasagna than you can store. Ask people if they'd store up that goodwill and maybe do a meal on a schedule. You might have one friend who can even organize the meal team. Another option is to ask people for gift cards to restaurants or meal delivery services for those nights when you just need a quick meal with no fuss.

Laundry: Start at home and speed up how fast your other kids can take over. Provide a small financial incentive if you need to. Or ask that friend or family member who really wants to help to come over on the weekend and be your laundry angel.

Errands: This is an easy and low-skill way for others to really help. Whether it's picking up prescriptions, shopping, taking siblings to activities, someone to drive around town and do things for you takes a huge load off you as the primary caregiver.

Gift Cards: A spin on errands would be money to have things delivered or done for a fee.

RESPITE CARE

Having someone watch your child can be tricky if their diagnosis is medically complex. That said, I spoke with parents who found nurses in their network who volunteered and could handle most medical needs.

Village Aid: Ask your friends, family, church members to adopt a schedule and give you a break. This could be a few hours to allow a night out with your spouse or the other kids. It might mean an hour to sit on your porch, read a book, or take a crazy-long hot shower or bath.

Tag-teaming: If you have a spouse, divide and conquer. Take turns spending time with the other kids.

Respite Programs: Many nonprofits recognize the need for a break and have programs as small as covering a few hours or as large as being able to take your child for a weekend. Ask if any such programs exist in your area.

Made in the USA
Coppell, TX
30 September 2024